JOSHUA RINARD

Oil & Fire

Encounter The God Who Still Speaks

Life SPRING
DESIGN

I dedicate this book to Jesus because He loved me first.

Contents

Preface   ii

 1   Awaken the Dove   1

 2   War of Two Kingdoms   11

 3   Missing Encounter   19

 4   Dark City   28

 5   The Mountain   39

 6   Hunger   49

 7   Fire   62

 8   Signals and Oil   72

 9   Promises in the Desert   81

10   Warfare Tactics   89

11   Cloud   104

12   Lightning   114

13   Thunder   124

14   Olive   134

You're Part of the Story   143

About the Author   144

Preface

If we were sitting down over coffee, I'd probably start by saying this isn't the book I ever thought I'd write. It's not filled with polished theology or bullet point strategies for becoming a better Christian. It's not about religious performance or trying harder to be good. This is something far more personal.

It's a journey of encounters and the pursuit of God's presence. Some moments are messy. Others are miraculous. All are real.

Over the years, I've come to believe that one of the most overlooked truths in the Church today is that God still speaks, and not just to spiritual leaders, pastors, or people with big platforms. He speaks to people like you and me.

This book came out of years of learning to recognize that voice, learning to host His presence, and discovering that encounters with God don't just happen on mountaintops or in worship services. They happen in deserts, in disappointment, and often when you least expect it.

Some of the stories in this book are wild. Some are deeply personal. But none of them are exaggerated. The writing is as authentic as I can make it. I'm not a professional editor or polished author, and I'm not trying to be. I'm comfortable with condensed thoughts and short bursts of ideas, even if they aren't fully expanded or tied neatly together. This is not about meeting anyone's expectations or crafting perfect stories. It's about saying what I believe He wants to say. I leave them unpolished, direct, and alive with the moments they carry.

In the early stages of this book, it was just me sitting with the Lord, writing down memories and moments, processing the past with Him. As I did, He began bringing answers to questions I'd carried for years. Some days I found myself in tears over moments I hadn't thought about in so long, because God had put His finger on something and wanted to talk about it.

Out of those conversations came what felt like a love letter, something He was weaving together with a golden thread. This book is my attempt to simply follow that thread the best I could, and it became one of the most powerful things I have ever done. I did it not just to tell a story, but to let the Holy Spirit meet me in the process. And now, I hope He will meet you too.

There Is More

I think a lot of us grew up with a version of God that lived in a box. A box built from rules, routines, and expectations of how He behaves. He stayed inside the lines, mostly quiet unless we did something wrong. But the longer I walk with Him, the more convinced I am that He is far bigger than any box. He is endlessly creative, always present and is personally invested in each of us.

Jesus didn't come to start a religion. He came to show the way into relationship with His Father. I believe this book will take you on a journey to rediscover who you were created to be, free, alive, and fully His.

I'm not writing from a stage or a title. I'm writing from lived experience shaped by God's relentless pursuit, and just as He pursues me, I believe that as you read, you'll encounter His presence in a whole new way. The Holy Spirit will awaken you to the reality that there is more... and that it is for you.

The Next Great Awakening

We are living in a time of great spiritual awakening. Magic and the supernatural are everywhere, in movies, culture, and media, where computer-generated worlds stretch far beyond our solar system. In this age, everything we see is often assumed to be fake before real. Yet beneath this, a generation is waking up hungry for something genuine, something real beyond the screens and illusions.

Our imaginations are being fueled like never before, and yet what we truly long for is not fantasy but reality, a reality greater than the natural world, one we all know deep down is true.

The days we live in demand more than surface-level belief or religious routine. We need transformed lives that walk in the Holy Spirit and demonstrate God's Kingdom with signs, wonders and miracles. The world around us seems to be growing darker now more than ever. However the truth is the enemy is only responding to the advancement of the Kingdom of God. God is on the move and He is waking people up. He is trying to save everyone and He is playing for keeps. The next great awakening is here. He is looking for hearts that are willing to say yes. Yes, to encounter Him and never be the same again. This is your invitation.

—Joshua Rinard

1

Awaken the Dove

"I saw the Spirit descending from heaven like a dove, and He remained upon Him."
   John 1:32 (NKJV)

Fire Tunnel

Walking through a crowd of people after a Sunday morning worship service. A large amount of leadership all lined up on either side of the exit like a receiving line with hands raised up making a tunnel like one might see at a sports game. It was the first time I had seen this kind of thing and didn't know what it was about. I was trying to get to the exit to avoid any uncomfortable conversations, but of course, the tunnel wrapped over the exit so the only way to leave was to pass through it or pull the fire alarm. Feeling a little uncomfortable, I waited for my turn. When it came I closed my eyes and began to walk through the tunnel making my 6'4" self as small as possible. As I passed by people started touching my shoulder and prayed, and occasionally they declared some sort of blessing. It was a practice of impartation.

I felt Him, and then I knew that the Lord had set me up.

The Holy Spirit began to move. I felt a fiery sensation shoot through my side as someone yelled "fire". The Holy Spirit coursed up my body as I took another step. Then, another voice cried out "fire" as they touched me, this time releasing a surge of electricity that jolted my heart. Another step and a third person touched the side of my temple and again I felt a rush of power and my defenses came down and my body reignited. My heart was no longer a small burning ember because I was alive again burning like it was always meant to. As I walked through the tunnel the Lord reminded me that I was His. When I got to the end of the tunnel a stranger asked to pray for me and I was done resisting. With no inside information He prayed specific things about me that only me and God knew. He mentioned specifics about forgotten dreams I hadn't thought about in years. The stranger was reading my mail in the best way possible. Jesus spoke to me deeply through this encounter and I knew my hiding was over. It's time that I come out of the cave.

Awakened

After this experience, I woke up realizing just how deeply I had been asleep. It was as if the Holy Spirit had flipped a switch and the intensity was permanently increased in me and on me. Although I had previously been filled with the Holy Spirit years before and do live with an awareness of His presence, this experience took me to a whole new level inviting me into a closer relationship with Him.

For me, the Holy Spirit generally feels like an inner river that flows inside me. I can pull on it with my heart and draw water from its well. I can find encouragement from Him and counsel and direction in life. However, when I went through this prayer tunnel I received a jump start. My past experiences with his presence that felt like oil, fire, and with electricity came back simultaneously as well as the memories attached to them. Instead of feeling overwhelmed with all kinds of questions, I felt a sense of completeness. Like I had come full circle and the time was finally here for this measure of Glory to be normal. I could not believe it took me so long to realize what God set out to do years earlier was supposed to be my normal. I neglected the standard Jesus set.

Dream - Are you Ready?

Around the same time, the Lord spoke to me through a dream. It started in my study room in front of my bookcase. It's full of spiritual books from my years of bible school and just pursuing God. In my dream, I pulled off the shelf a white 3-ring binder and opened it. I saw clear plastic pockets like what you would put collectible cards in. Only in each pocket was a pile of multicolored money. The money reminded me of British pounds and was in piles of 10s and piles of 100s. I flipped through the pages of the collection I cherished. I said in the dream "I wonder if there are any 1000 dollar notes?" Then I heard a voice say "with God all things are possible." As I watched the 10s and 100s started shifting into 1000-pound notes. Then I heard a knock at the door and ran to the window and looked out at the visitor. My friend Sam from England pulled up in his smart car like the one He drove when I lived in England. He pulled up with his window down like He was coming to pick me up and asked me a question. He said, "Are you ready?." Then I woke up.

This dream is packed full of symbolism that needs unpacking. The binder on the shelf represents the past valuable history with God that I stored on my shelf for safekeeping. White three-ring binder is the trinity. Money is treasure and testimonies. Each pile is stored like a precious memory or revelation. The 10s and 100s represent the value of the encounter placed either by me or by God. Money in a good context generally means favor, anointing, or influence. Then at the sound of His word multiplication happens. There is more to the dream. My friend's name is Samuel, which means "The Lord hears you", and He asked me "if I was ready." All while indicating He was there to pick me up. The dream is very profound to me because it's like God said I see your past, and I'm going to use those treasures and multiply them. I'm here to pick you up, get you ready and accomplish my words that don't fail. "With God, all things are possible." Matthew 19:26 (NLT)

Even if we forget what God said He doesn't. He remembers His words and knows how to correct our course and empower us to move forward in the right direction. When He says something, the words carry everything needed to accomplish them. Are you ready for what the Lord wants to do with you?

I believe the Lord wants to multiply your encounters far beyond what you expect. He wants to increase your favor and intimacy with Him.

In this season His presence was more tangible than ever before and I had an expectation for more. I felt the Holy Spirit moving around me and on me, it was fluttering like a dove.

The Dove

Jesus lives with the Holy Spirit in Him and upon Him. In *John 1:32 (NASB)* John said *"I have seen the Spirit descending as a dove out of heaven, and it remained upon Him."* John intentionally told us that the Holy Spirit in the form of a dove remained upon Jesus. The dove didn't temporarily show up to perform miracles. It lived life with Him. The Holy Spirit was there when He slept. It was there when He ate. The dove was there when Jesus walked into the temple and saw people selling doves for money. (see John 2:16) I believe He took that form to reveal to us part of His nature. Doves aren't pigeons. They are calm, gentle, and meek. They are super sensitive and I believe God wanted us to know that about Him. What if every choice you made needed to honor the Presence resting on you? How would your life begin to adjust in order to keep Him there?

As my experiences in this season grew I noticed the Spirit would rest on me. I would feel different sensations of His presence that were layered in my previous encounters. Feelings of Water, Oil, and Fire can all be present on my head. I can feel Him shift around throughout the day and the easiest way to describe Him is like a dove flew in and is making a nest on my head. I feel the ebb and flow of anointing oil. Similar to syrup running down my head. Then sometimes He shifts and I feel a flickering flame. I feel the fire often on my forehead. It's not hot, but I feel the flame move to the sound of worship in whatever form that takes. It's almost like a dove standing up and rustling its feathers, rotating around, and sitting back down to get comfortable. Sometimes He spreads His wings and I feel a heightened sense of lightness and confidence, almost as if everything stands at attention. I have moments where He taps on my head, ear, or shoulder as if to get my attention. His presence pursues me throughout the day, and I can usually feel Him stirring me and other times encouraging me to linger longer in the secret place.

The Ark and the Dove

The truth around the dove can be seen much earlier in scripture in the days of Noah.

After the flood, while Noah and his family were still on the ark, Noah opened the top window and sent out a dove to look for new life and a place to land. The scripture says *"But the dove found no resting place for the sole of her foot, and she returned to him into the ark, because the waters were on the face of the whole earth. So he put out his hand and took her and brought her to himself into the ark. Then he waited another seven days and again sent the dove out of the ark. And the dove came back to him in the evening, and behold, in her mouth was a freshly plucked olive leaf. So Noah knew that the waters had receded from the earth. Then he waited another seven days and sent out the dove, which did not return to him anymore."* Genesis 8:9-12 (NKJV)

Jesus is the ark that everyone gets saved in, and the dove is the Holy Spirit. The dove is looking for a place to not only land but to live. When He lands on you does He stay? When you have to do normal life, does your heart first take into account the dove?

When I pray, worship, and spend time with the Lord the presence increases. When life gets busy He can fade into the background a bit and I become less aware. He promises to never leave us but He can easily hide inside us when we stop looking at Jesus or entertain darkness. I will admit on many occasions the dove has hidden and I had to get to know what He likes and doesn't like if there ever was a chance He would remain manifest. The Holy Spirit has a personality. He feels things. What you think, say, and do matters to Him.

Personality

One day I was at work and I was carrying His presence on me. I was very busy but I could feel the dove sitting there on my head. He was quiet. Not fluttering much. Not very excited, just resting. As the work day progressed I noticed He hadn't moved much so I took a moment and engaged by asking Him a question. "Lord, what's going on? You're quiet, are you ok today?"

He responded with, "I'm lonely"

I said, "lonely?... Lord. There have to be millions of people talking to you right now. Why are you feeling that way?"

He said, "They aren't you. There is no one like you."

The Holy Spirit wants time with us. He values our friendship much more than we give Him credit. He is looking for people who will respond to His daily invitation. Jesus lives in you so the Holy Spirit should feel safe to not only land but remain. He can fly anywhere He wants, but I want Him to find me when He wants intimacy. We should carry a sense of responsibility to protect and value that connection no matter what it costs us personally. What is it going to take for the dove to remain?

Why Tangible

If you have a relationship where you only talk on the phone then it's not a very close one. You can talk about all kinds of things, but for the relationship to go further there has to be a point where you actually meet face-to-face. Eventually, you need to hold a hand or give a hug. Look into their eyes and connect more deeply. How many times do we call God up on our phone and try to leave a message instead of inviting Him to come over for dinner? Calls are valuable but they don't replace a tangible relationship. In the gospel of Matthew, Jesus said that He would always be with us. That's not just a nice thing to say.

Jesus is available to get to know. He will come over for dinner and not only speak to you but He will touch you. He will tear down your walls and completely rebuild you. If all you want is a long-distance relationship, then

He will meet you there, but if you don't know His presence you may not know Him. God is not far, He became a man so you could touch Him. The presence of the Holy Spirit is Him, present. It is His face and His voice. You know when Jesus walks into the room because everything that's not part of His kingdom bows.

My Friend Jack

Just like in the days of Noah, the Holy Spirit is looking for places to land. (See Gen 8). On this particular day, I had an opportunity. I was aware of the Holy Spirit's presence fluttering a bit like any other day. I pulled up to a customer's home to make a delivery. I'll call him Jack for the sake of this story. Jack was an older man, probably in his 70s. He was a kind person but I didn't know him very well. I dropped my package off and he was sitting down on a chair clearly in discomfort. We got to talking and he mentioned he had excruciating back pain.

I felt compassion for him and I asked him if he would let me pray for him. He said he believed in Jesus and has for years. Realizing I was talking to a believer I relaxed a bit. We bowed our heads, I held out my hands and we prayed. I told him to wait a minute for the Holy Spirit. Honestly, I wanted to see if I could feel him move. I waited about 8 seconds or so and I felt him. I felt the Holy Spirit flutter and increase in intensity on my head and then on my hands. I then prayed from that place, just a simple prayer for healing, I rebuked the pain and released the presence to the best my faith could do. Opening my eyes I realized Jack started crying. I asked him what was going on. He said he felt a heat go across his back. He has never felt that before. He had pain in his back every day for 34 years. The pain was gone. He got up and walked around thanking God.

The Holy Spirit should always have permission to interrupt your plans. He may pull you into a divine moment where He shares His heart for someone else and all you need to do is follow.

How to Carry the Dove

Be open to discovering the Holy Spirit even if His expression doesn't fit inside your expectations. The Lord reveals Himself differently to each person. This is not a complete list by any means but some people feel Him in their hearts, some understand Him through their minds, some see Him with their eyes, some hear Him with their ears, and some simply know Him. He also reveals Himself through visions and dreams. *He promised to do infinitely more than your greatest request. Ephesians 3:20 (TPT).* You may encounter Him in alignment with your gifting or even your calling, but sometimes the Lord may surprise you with something unexpected. Be fully present and aware of His physical presence, even if it exceeds your previous expectations. Let Him be God and just enjoy what He wants to do because it's not like you're going to change Him. You might as well be the one that changes.

How do we become a place where the dove lands and makes its home? Accepting Christ into your heart and becoming baptized in the Holy Spirit is just an early invitation to start walking in intimacy with God. Spending time with Him builds a place for Him to land. You still have to live it out daily through all the ups and downs of life. Sometimes it's easy to connect to the Holy Spirit and other times He can seem very quiet.

The dryness can feel real. I've physically and mentally tired myself out with singing, dancing, and worshiping. The thing that His presence connected through the day before sometimes wouldn't work the next day. Realize He's not a vending machine. You can't insert a worship song like a transaction and out comes an encounter. Jesus is faithful and loves showing up, but sometimes He is unpredictable and doesn't always show up how you expect.

I think it's those quiet times that reveal our heart condition. It makes sense that while in His glorious presence, you feel His pleasure and are empowered to do the things that honor Him. However, do you only think and do the right thing when His presence is on you? Shouldn't time in His presence impart to you transformation into a person who thinks and acts like his Creator? Are you a pretender that drinks His river freely and refuses to change or are you a son of God? What kind of person are you going to be when you feel nothing?

Regardless of how we feel, our posture must stay fixed on Christ. Dry times don't bother me as much as they used to. Because when you have found Jesus, He becomes the one thing everything else points to. He is the single greatest treasure of all time.

With His help, I adjust my heart, remove religious duty and try something new. Sometimes I just sit on the ground in silence and listen. Meditate on a verse and simply wait. Sometimes I go for a walk and I try to be creative with my time. He likes to hide His word or truth like a buried treasure ready for me to find. I abide in Him and He abides in me and when I find what the Holy Spirit is highlighting... I lean in closer. I trust Him to show up because His word says He will and because I'm convinced that He likes to be with me. I think the most important thing about being a landing place is to be a place of honest worship; honest worship builds a deeper connection with Him.

My focus has shifted to cultivating an atmosphere of worship that is so attractive to Him that He accepts my invitation because there are no strings attached. Just me and Him.

Are You Ready?

Are you ready for the Lord to encounter you in a way you never thought was possible? Are you one of those people who will draw close to Jesus and receive what He has to give? His presence needs to rest on us and around us to such a degree that people get touched by simply being near us.

We need to raise our expectations of what God's presence can do. We need to be a people with our gaze so fixed on Jesus that we don't move until He shows up, and when He does we then follow. This is essential because if the Lord doesn't show up then we have missed the point entirely.

The revival we need rests on those who protect His presence. They are the ones that Jesus likes to be with. They don't compromise for position or influence, and they can't be bought. Their fuel is the love of God, and they don't accept anything less than the reality of His kingdom. With Jesus they heal the sick, raise the dead, cleanse diseases, and cast out demons. They are unique in that they carry their revival wherever they go. They understand while abiding in Jesus, they are just as powerful in this world as He is. (see 1 John 4:17) They exhibit unwavering focus and determination as they slay giants, set people free, and influence culture. Their words silence storms and their prayers move mountains. They expect greater things today, they fight for tomorrow and they give their life for something greater than themselves. They live in hope, expecting Him to turn the world right side up.

2

War of Two Kingdoms

"You saw me before I was born. Every day of my life was recorded in your book. Every moment was laid out before a single day had passed." Psalm 139:16 (NLT)

Encounter

There are moments in life when the Holy Spirit shifts and Jesus walks into the room. He is the bridegroom who is passionately pursuing us, His bride. Jesus sent the Holy Spirit to live in us and upon us, to draw us deeper into knowing Him. He is all about representing His Father and bringing heaven to earth *(see Matthew 6:10)* When the Holy Spirit comes and we recognize it we are given a divine invitation to encounter Him. Encounters in His presence often include things like creative ideas, healing, visions, dreams, wisdom, or even knowledge. Angels can even be involved in a variety of ways. Encounters shift things in our nature and leave a deposit of truth that has the potential to grow as we carry it.

We were made to live in His presence close to His heart. The closeness fosters personal sustaining revival, where signs, wonders, and miracles are a common happening. These kinds of manifestations happen through intimacy with Jesus. Christians were once known as people who had been with Jesus because the fruit they produced were actual miracles and changed lives. Jesus is longing for a people who will linger longer in His presence. He wants to know you on a level that you didn't even know was possible, and when He opens the door He sets the precedence of what is possible. All things are possible!

"Never doubt God's mighty power to work in you and accomplish all this. He will achieve infinitely more than your greatest request, your most unbelievable dream, and exceed your wildest imagination! He will outdo them all, for his miraculous power constantly energizes you." Ephesians 3:20 (TPT)

Afraid of the Dark

When I was a little boy, about 7 years old, my family was living in Elko, Nevada. Elko is a small desert mining town. My dad worked in lumber, working long hard hours to prove Himself; while my mom was working hard raising five kids. They are both heroes in their individual way. We had a modest home and I shared a room with my brother Zach, who at the time was about a year old.

I don't know how or when it started but nighttime was the worst time for me. My nights were full of sleeplessness and fear. I'd hear voices and see things in my imagination, and in the physical, that would keep me gripped in terror. Each night was a battlefield and I was completely unaware of how to fight back. I don't know exactly how long it lasted but this season was at least several months. I would call for my mom and she would often come to hold and help comfort me. I would ask her not to leave until I'd fallen asleep and then hope not to wake until morning. This worked, but of course, moms can't do that every night.

On one particular night, as fear took its grip on me, I called out for my mom. Baby Zach was sound asleep, and I couldn't yell any louder without waking Him. Again I called out for mom and nobody came to the rescue. I had this overwhelming sense of fear, loneliness, and powerlessness. As I lay on my stomach trying to hide my face from any kind of trigger, with tears dripping on my pillow I said a prayer. *"Jesus if you are real... I need you to help me. I'm afraid."* I remember it like it was yesterday. Immediately a presence poured over me and I felt a hand rest on my back. An overwhelming sense of peace came upon me and there was nothing like His touch. Jesus the Prince of Peace came and the fear left. I heard Him begin to speak over my life and future, and as His words came and peace overtook me, I did what only a little boy would do, and I fell asleep.

The Storm

In Mark chapter 6 the disciples of Jesus had an interesting experience trying to cross the sea of Galilee. God responded to them through Jesus and what He did had a profound impact on them.

"Immediately after this, Jesus insisted that his disciples get back into the boat and head across the lake to Bethsaida, while he sent the people home. After telling everyone goodbye, he went up into the hills by Himself to pray.

Late that night, the disciples were in their boat in the middle of the lake, and Jesus was alone on land. He saw that they were in serious trouble, rowing hard and struggling against the wind and waves. About three o'clock in the morning Jesus came toward them, walking on the water. He intended to go past them, but when they saw Him walking on the water, they cried out in terror, thinking he was a ghost. They were all terrified when they saw Him.

But Jesus spoke to them at once. 'Don't be afraid,' he said. 'Take courage! I am here!' Then he climbed into the boat, and the wind stopped. They were totally amazed. Mark 6:45-51 (NLT)

What a spectacular encounter with the Prince of Peace. Jesus sends the disciples off so He can spend time with His Father. The disciples were a group of mostly seasoned fishermen who were familiar with this specific body of water. They knew what it meant to weather a storm, so this must have been a spectacular storm as they were struggling for their lives.

The gospel of Mark says that Jesus saw that they were in serious trouble. Despite the dark evening, and the probable chill of wind and rain blowing, the Holy Spirit which rests with Jesus, most likely told Him His guys were in trouble. Then Jesus comes to the rescue by just walking out into the chaos. The storm knew who Jesus was and in the same way, so do our storms. Jesus is the source of true peace.

Jesus cared that His disciples not only made it across but how they made it. Jesus said

"'Don't be afraid,' he said. 'Take courage! I am here!' Then he climbed into the boat, and the wind stopped." Mark 6:50–51

Jesus spoke faith into His friends. He revealed His authority and then removed the fear. Once He spoke into their lives. He stepped into their boat just like He stepped into my bedroom. The disciples were amazed; they didn't know the sheer magnitude of who was with them, and what He gave them. Neither did I.

The morning after Jesus showed up in my room, I overslept and my mother had to wake me. The day was already bright and I had a lingering feeling of my encounter the night before. I told my mother that I prayed to Jesus and He came to visit me. I asked her to tell me who He was. I had never met Jesus before, but I knew my mother was a believer and she said His name on occasion. She explained the simplicity of the gospel and I prayed to accept Jesus into my heart and life. I didn't know what the implications of this were. I just knew He helped me.

"Everyone who calls on the name of the Lord will be saved." Romans 10:13 (NLT)

Encountering His Love

"For God so loved the world that he sent Jesus." John 3:16 (NLT)

The encounter I had with the Lord's peace overcoming my fear went the way of most things. I forgot about it. Life went on and the experience became lost. But it wasn't too long before God revealed Himself again.

A couple of years later I was about 9, and my home was on the edge of an elementary school's property. I was out rollerblading with a friend and ended up following along in my friend's attempt to play a trick on some much older junior high kids. The prank was something super clever like filling the kid's shoes with playground bark. I mainly observed as my friend caused mischief which didn't last long because of course one of the teenage boys caught us and then proceeded to bully us. What seemed like a relatively harmless trick turned into a verbal attack back at us. Moments later my friend bolted away on his skates leaving me behind to face the fury. With a barrage of unkind words being shot at me and my level of fear growing I began to skate home as fast as I could. The bully chased me all the way home, yelling at me. That was one of the first times in my life I felt the same fear in the daytime that I felt at night. It was terrifying. My adrenaline was pumping intensely and I was doing everything I could to keep from crying. With all my strength I bolted into my open garage and jumped into an old recliner and spun around to conceal my escape. Thankfully, The bully didn't follow me into my garage and I sat in that red recliner panting out of breath terrified about what I just experienced. I felt fear pressing on my chest. I felt betrayed by my friend and misunderstood by my pursuer. With my heart pounding I closed my eyes and said a simple prayer, "Jesus…. I'm afraid". That's all it took for Him to show up.

The Holy Spirit poured on me like water. His presence started on my head and began to pour downward. I recognized the feeling from somewhere familiar and peaceful. Then I heard Him: "*I am here*". The shaking fear I felt was overshadowed and disintegrated by the love of God. I had forgotten about my last encounter a couple of years earlier, but now I remembered the peace. I remembered the feeling of His presence falling on me permeating my feelings and filling my heart. From that encounter in my room to this moment in my garage, He hadn't left me. He loved me and reminded me that I didn't have to be afraid. He was there, and He was stronger than everything else. That affected me in a profound way and started me on a path to know Him through His word and through experience.

"And *this is eternal life: that they know you, the only true God, and Jesus Christ, whom you have sent.*" John 17:3 (NLT)

Two Kingdoms - Dark and Light

These moments revealed to me that there is a spiritual contrast between two opposing kingdoms, Dark and Light. On earth, darkness tends to be louder and seems to demand all the attention. It's full of showmanship, trickery, and distraction. Its focus is to steal, kill and destroy us. The primary weapon of the enemy is fear, mostly because it has nothing else to stand on. If the enemy manage to keep us in fear then we're not living by faith in God. Fear is not the absence of faith, it is just faith in the wrong kingdom. The enemy uses fear tactics to keep people distracted from the truth of who they are made to be.

Dark Tactic

One tactic the enemy tries on children is using fear to convince them to close off from all spiritual things because it's too scary or dangerous, or not "real". If the enemy can successfully convince kids to disconnect from the unknown things then they can succeed in cutting children off from spiritual things early on which is where we build our identity and discover who we are. Then we're positioned to be influenced by other lies. Such as; "God doesn't care or God is not real.." "If He was real why would He care about you?" When we believe a lie or give into fear we empower the enemy to hijack our minds and use it against us. The truth is the enemy has no authority, and it tries to convince us that we don't either which is further from the truth. If the enemy keeps us afraid of spiritual things then we will close off our hearts to the things God is saying about us. How can we hear the good things He's saying to us if we aren't listening? If we can't hear what God is saying about us, who will we become and whose kingdom will we subsequently live in?

Kingdom of Peace

The light is the kingdom of heaven, It's full of faith and God's goodness. God desires us to draw into a greater relationship with the Holy Spirit which connects us to Jesus and in turn His Father. God's heart isn't to manipulate or control, His heart is to walk with us as we discover why we were made. Encounters are those moments where He steps into our world and draws us into His. In this story, He stepped into my room and my garage and gave me a gift. Jesus said *"I am leaving you with a gift—peace of mind and heart. And the peace I give is a gift the world cannot give. So don't be troubled or afraid."* John 15:27 (NLT)

The world's definition of peace is a lack of turmoil but that's not the right picture. The peace of God doesn't passively ease tension; it establishes order, and overcomes everything. It is the presence of the Holy Spirit given by God because of what Jesus did. His peace conquers any atmosphere. It's given to us as a gift, but as with any gift, we have to open it and use it.

This struggle with fear and the unknown took time to overcome. The peace did silence the voices and the things I saw, but they kept coming back until I learned to let His peace silence me. The peace removed the inner turmoil and aligned my heart to connect to the power which is greater than the darkness. When I feel a moment of fear I remember what He gave me on that night and the atmosphere shifts around me because of what I carry.

One way to recognize what the Lord is saying to you is to see what the enemy is trying to steal. The Lord wanted to use that time of the day to connect with me. He can come at any time of course but it was in that weak place where He set up His throne and began to teach me. The enemy watched night after night as Jesus and the Holy Spirit showed up in the Twilight hours. The darkness eventually gives up when they realize that I'm wasting their time. Living in a relationship with God is just that much better than living in fear. His powerful peace has had the single greatest impact on my life and I will wield it for the rest of my life.

God's Solution

These encounters happened because of His grace. I didn't do anything to earn it. Grace is not only undeserved favor but the power to do something you could not do before. What people fail to realize is He doesn't take back His grace. When Jesus sets precedence in your life He is inviting you to live within the revelation of that grace at that measure of Glory. It should now be the floor you stand on. He doesn't want to just step in and change a moment and let things go back to normal. He intentionally alters you so that you are never the same again.

To this day I get the most visitations from Him in the night hours. Nearly every night, as I lay in bed the weight of the Holy Spirit rests on my head and face. It has for years. It's encouraging at the end of the day and it feels like the Holy Spirit is just loving me. It's in those moments that I ask questions, watch for answers, and listen for His voice.

The Holy Spirit reminds me that Jesus is with me. When Jesus steps into our boat He has a way about Him that makes storms bend their knees, then He shows us how to do it ourselves.

"I have told you all this so that you may have peace in me. Here on earth, you will have many trials and sorrows. But take heart, because I have overcome the world." John 16:33 (NLT)

"In peace I will lie down and sleep, for you alone, O Lord will keep me safe." Psalm 4:8 (NLT)

"Indeed, he who watches over Israel never slumbers or sleeps. The Lord Himself watches over you! The Lord stands beside you as your protective shade." Psalm 121:4–5 (NLT)

3

Missing Encounter

"For John baptized with water, but in just a few days you will be baptized with the Holy Spirit." Acts 1:5 (NLT)

Summer Camp

At the age of 13, I went to a youth church summer camp in McCall, Idaho, and I thought I was about to have a life changing encounter with the Holy Spirit.

The atmosphere was electric. During one of the evening services, the guest speaker began talking about the Holy Spirit. He read verse after verse about how Jesus promised to send an Advocate who would live in us and never leave us. He said this promise was still for us today, and I believed Him.

Jesus said *"I will ask the Father, and he will give you another Advocate, who will never leave you. He is the Holy Spirit, who leads into all truth. The world cannot receive Him, because it isn't looking for Him and doesn't recognize Him. But you know Him because he lives with you now and later will be in you."*

John 14:16–17 (NLT)

Jesus promised to send the Holy Spirit to live in us and one sign of this is speaking in an unknown tongue or another language. In its simplest form, speaking in unknown tongues refers to a deeply personal prayer language that exists between you and God. The guest speaker then asked us. If you want to be filled with the Holy Spirit and speak in tongues then raise your hand and come forward. That sounded pretty nice, but I felt uncomfortable raising my hand because I didn't want to be the only one. When I saw the other hands being raised the pressure dropped and I responded. The prayer team started ministering to us to receive the Holy Spirit. As the team went down the line praying for people one by one they began to speak in their unique language.

Seemed easy enough but when it was my turn nothing came out. All I had was good old American English! I felt a lot of pressure from people around me to stop thinking and just open my mouth and let God fill it. I was self-conscious and uncomfortable so I disconnected. I was stuck in my head, and I didn't know what else to do. I already had the Holy Spirit but not the prayer language. I began to turn inward and ask God what was wrong with me.

While this was happening the leadership kept encouraging everyone to worship and press into God. With the band playing in the background the Holy Spirit took things to another measure of Glory and started encountering kids all over the room. It was not long before it became apparent that I was the only person still standing on his feet trying to connect to God. The last thing I wanted was to stand out but that's what happened.

Eventually, I wandered over to the guest speaker who prayed for me and encouraged me. I sat down next to him on the edge of the stage facing the crowd and we just watched. It didn't matter that I was there because it seemed like everyone else in the room was being encountered by the Holy Spirit in very unique ways.

Many kids were laughing hysterically, some were rolling on the floor like they were drunk. I heard a few people with slurred speech talking about conversations they just had with angels. Something was changing in the atmosphere. The pastor and I just watched God move. After the extended service ended we were dismissed. I stepped outside into the night and walked toward my cabin. I had questions.

Missing Encounter

Do you ever feel like God doesn't show up when you want or the way you want? You try to check all the boxes, you sing all the songs and you just can't seem to break through the lid that you didn't know was there. People around you are experiencing God in their own unique way but you are seemingly in the same place you were years ago. What do you do?

Resources of Heaven

Why can it take a long time to get answers to prayer? Are the delays we experience in unanswered prayer because God was slow to respond? Is our personal faith affecting the outcome? Was it a matter of just time or are there more layers of abstraction that have to be worked out?

Let's explore a bit and consider it might be more complicated than we think. God always answers prayers. He just doesn't always answer them in our time frame. Daniel is a great example of this. When he had a vision in Daniel 10:13 he went into fasting and prayer for an interpretation. He waited three weeks before he got an answer. An angel showed up and indicated that his prayer was answered right away and he had been trying to get to Daniel for 21 days. This angel, who is known to be Gabriel, a high-ranking archangel, got stopped by a spiritual power en route. The angel had to change strategy and go get Michael the archangel to fight so he could get through enemy lines. The moment you pray, Jesus deploys angels to deliver the word of the Lord for your situation. This gives some indication of a hierarchy of spiritual beings, and systems in place that might be factored into how heaven interacts with earth.

When you pray, does God hear it immediately, or do the sound waves need to travel to His ears? When He makes a decision, it stands to reason it most likely includes other factors like a time and a place. If the time is delayed, then there might be some prerequisites He wants you to go through before you can handle His response. For the sake of this exploration, let's ponder a very basic system. Let's assume the Godhead makes the decision right away and speaks, which is pretty mainstream Christianity to believe that. Are His words for your situation recorded by a scribe? The word is most likely given to a dispatcher who sorts what angel or team it should go to. Assuming the messenger angel was actually present and not getting push notifications while on other assignments in other locations, the messenger supernaturally uses a portal to get from that specific area of heaven to the earthly realm. Then the messenger has to go through conflicting spiritual powers, thrones, and dominions in the second heaven to get into the same physical realm I'm in. Then the messenger angel temporarily bends the laws of our physics to travel to and communicate to us a spiritual message we understand.

This exploration is very simplified because it's not taking into account whether or not the messenger angel might need other angels to help.

People don't have the same gifts. Why would we assume angels do? A "PR"(public relations) angel that has the message might deliver it because they are faster or more eloquent than other angels, but may need help from an angel that can do an impartation of a healing which might include a manifestation like heat or electricity to accompany the message. Maybe they are dependent on waiting for the Holy Spirit for the timing. The angel also might need to consult with our guardian angel to determine the ways we best receive messages. Maybe letters and numbers on a license plate are not the best way to receive life-changing instructions. It wouldn't surprise me if the Lord lets angels be creative in how they get the job done.

There is also this idea that God already knows what we need before we ask for it. If He already knows what we are going to ask, and knows all the outcomes then does He dispatch resources in advance? I'd say sometimes He does. The scripture has times where the angel goes ahead of people to make their mission successful. I also think our measure of faith at the moment might be a factor that changes the outcome. We need to realize more things are going on than we see. Just imagining any kind of infrastructure complicates the answer to the question of how long does it take to get an answer to prayer?

Considering the environment I was in during this service I would rule out the possibility of my missed encounter being a resource issue. It would only take one manifestation in the room to prove God and His angels were present, and as I mentioned earlier there were plenty of kids encountering the Lord.

When Striving Ends

"For this reason, the Lord is still waiting to show his favor to you so he can show you his marvelous love. He waits to be gracious to you. He sits on his throne ready to show mercy to you. For Yahweh is the Lord of justice, faithful to keep his promises. Overwhelmed with bliss are all who will entwine their hearts in Him, waiting for Him to help them." Isaiah 30:18 (TPT)

Occasionally, when your desires are not fulfilled immediately, it provides a chance to cultivate a seed and make arrangements for the future. The purpose behind this is to prepare you for an encounter that hasn't happened yet. It's important to Him that you can receive His message in a way where you can carry the gravity of it.

There is a mystery in life around unanswered prayer in that the moment you let go... seems to be directly related to the moment you receive what you have been waiting for.

I still remember looking up at the stars on that warm summer night. There was a light breeze that shook the tall trees that surrounded the camp. Kids were heading off to their cabins and I detoured to a nearby clearing for some quiet time. My heart had questions that faded out of importance and I watched silently. I knew He was with me because He always has been. We looked at the stars together and enjoyed each other's company. He connected with me and I started praying in tongues right there in the dark.

I pursued Him in the service and prayed the prayers, sang the songs, made my requests, and did everything that was asked of me by the leaders. But when all the striving was over and done, He met me when it wasn't about the request. There was something about that moment under the stars that He wanted to just be between me and Him.

When you're waiting for God to meet you in a certain area and it feels as though you've missed Him, you have to trust. Trust that He is working out the details and the timing. The promises He is fulfilling often stretch across generations. God is in the business of doing exactly what He said He would do. You are not in the same place you use to be. You're already on the journey of discovering everything He has planned for you. His timing rarely matches ours, but the dream in your heart is His dream, because He planted it there from the beginning.

Between

That encounter was a marking moment where I knew God did something incredible in me. Because of the unique timing of the encounter, it made me always wonder "what in the world happened that night?" It was several years later before I stopped looking at the event through insecurity and asked what God was doing. The question wasn't why did I miss my encounter in the service... The better question is what was God doing in the service that He wanted me to see?

Remember how I was sitting on the stage watching the movements of the Holy Spirit? He orchestrated an unusual moment for me to witness all kinds of manifestations that I had never seen before. Watching expanded the possibility that God expresses Himself in different ways than just speaking in tongues. All the encounters He was doing were unique and individually tailored for each person. God wanted to encounter people and He wanted me to see it. He didn't skip me, He gave me a special assignment which was to watch Him work.

Sometimes it's not about getting what you want, but it's about the journey of discovering what He wants. God is interested in those moments between our prayers and His answers. Those are the moments that develop the relationship.

God in a Box

The fulfillment of my request was postponed and I was given the assignment to witness the Holy Spirit encounter people. I just didn't know at the time. Through this, I realized that God intended for me to experience Him in a more intimate and personal manner, beyond the confines of a traditional service. It was a deliberate attempt to challenge and break the religious box that I had placed Him in.

When you put God in a box you approach your relationship as an outline of behavioral traits and miss the life changing power and intimacy He offers. Most people, even believers, don't realize how real and tangible He is. The majority of individuals are content with the existence of God as long as He stays at a distance. They prefer to be comfortable with Him living out of sight in a proverbial box, labeled, measured, and placed on a shelf for another time. This kind of person accepts God on their terms. They want Him to answer their prayers like He's a magical genie and stay quiet when He asks for us to change. They complain about the bad like it's His fault and give Him no credit for the good. They're OK with God as long as He stays out of their way. No matter how you try to package Him, God can't be contained. Father God wants it personal which is why He doesn't live in a box anymore, He lives in hearts.

The traditional religious structure is not a bad thing. It can just be overemphasized to the point of replacing the spontaneity of the person of the Holy Spirit. The issue is we can put God in a religious box and by faith diminish our expectation of what God can do for us on a personal level. Then He has to break the box so He can be seen as He is. We want God to accept us as we are but we fail to accept Him as He is. If we did then when the Holy Spirit manifests around us we would not feel uncomfortable but instead open to Him doing the thing He does. Touch people. His priority is not distance but close proximity.

God did all kinds of supernatural things recorded in scripture that were strange. He gave Samson superhuman strength enough to slay thousands of men. Moses participated in dozens of miracles including parting the Red Sea and meeting with God Himself. In the new testament, on the day of Pentecost, The Holy Spirit was poured out like visible fire. Which made the disciples sound and look drunk. We haven't even included the things Jesus did. John said *"Jesus did countless things that I haven't included here. And if every one of his works were written down and described one by one, I suppose that the world itself wouldn't have enough room to contain the books that would have to be written!"* (See John 21:25 TPT). There is no shortage of God showing off in special ways to draw people closer to knowing His heart.

He might fill people with joy so much they can't contain their laughter. He might place His presence on a person so heavy they fall on the ground. He might just reach into a heart and mend brokenness or even physically heal someone. There is no limit to what God does and what we can discover in Him. Just when we think we got Him boxed up He has no problem redefining the relationship boundaries of what is possible. All things are possible with God. When we begin to believe it, that's when the box shatters into a million pieces.

The Holy Spirit has many different expressions but believers have no idea how large the grid is. We need to avoid diminishing God into a single quantifiable manifestation. Limiting what He is like shrinks our faith and dims our eyesight. How can we believe to receive big miracles if all our expectations are small? How will we accept His subtle invitations into deeper experiences if we won't get out of the toddler pool? If we never embrace anything uncomfortable then we may never do anything incredible. The only things worth doing are found in participating in what He is doing. Remember He said *"You didn't choose me. I chose you." John 15:16. (MSG)*

Relevant Relationship

We have the Holy Spirit to guide us into knowing Jesus and His Father. He pursues a relationship with us. Closeness wrapped in honesty, love, faith, and grounded in His true reality. He prefers closeness that He can only have with a true friend. He has many servants trying to keep the rules and trying to stay inside the box. What He doesn't have is many friends, who will go deep with Him and stay there for as long as He wants. He has special moments picked that are tailor fit just for you. Although we don't always get to choose the time or place, we do get to pick our posture. Our stance becomes the landing pad for Heaven to invade earth. Get ready and watch for Him. Because if you look for Him, then you will see Him.

At my summer camp, I heard the wind blowing through huge trees as I gazed at the beautiful starry sky. Some of my most intimate moments with God are looking at the stars. The night sky reminds me of just how vast and brilliant God is. It gives me perspective on my life and makes me marvel and wonder. With everything going on in the universe He must value people, in that He would choose to live and make a home with us. He waited thousands of years to have a relationship with you, He's not going to waste it.

I had longed for an encounter in the service. I didn't get it the way I expected. But He met me under the stars, quietly, powerfully, in a way that was unmistakably personal.

And yet I know not every story wraps up that neatly. Maybe you're still standing in the middle of the room, watching others get what you've prayed for. Maybe your breakthrough still feels delayed. If that's you, don't give up. Sometimes it feels like we've been skipped, but God wastes nothing, He gets you ready. Even when nothing is happening on the surface, God is moving. He's preparing a moment that is tailor made for you. So stay expectant and watch for Him. Because if you keep looking, you will find Him.

"And everyone present was filled with the Holy Spirit and began speaking in other languages, as the Holy Spirit gave them this ability." Acts 2:4 (NLT)

"And these signs will accompany those who believe: In my name they will drive out demons; they will speak in new tongues" Mark 16:17 (NIV)

4

Dark City

In 2004, I was attending a very liberal art college in San Francisco and found myself in a dark place in my walk with God. Just as I woke from sleep I heard the sound of epic sword fighting in the atmosphere around my room. I heard the sound of a large fan or propeller pushing the air around just on the edge of my ears. It was clear at first but as I woke it faded behind the sounds of city life. I had an impression that there must be some sort of spiritual warfare going on in my room. I prayed for a few minutes just to be safe. Later that day my mother called me and one of the things she mentioned was that she had an urgency to pray for me that same morning. That is when I remembered hearing the spiritual activity just before waking up. I don't know exactly why I heard it, but I assumed it was to get my attention so that I could participate in the outcome.

Worship

I reached over and grabbed my acoustic guitar. I've taken it with me in many seasons. There is something about it that reminds me of where I came from. Worship was the first key to unlocking what God deposited in me years before.

My mother taught me the value of worship and what it does to the person who participates. I saw it modeled when she went through hard moments. She would get on her piano and she would unlock something supernatural in the room that would change the way she handled situations. She led by example and instilled in me the importance of worshiping God.

I don't always know what to pray for, but I can always worship. I began to play to the Lord. Praise and worship was the major factor that allowed me to live in that spiritually dark environment yet still let my burdens go, feel a sense of His presence, and focus on my assignments. When I worship I have this sense that I can escape my present reality and enter into a better one. One full of hope and freedom.

As the music faded, my focus turned from worship, back to my dorm room. It was a completely different environment than where I grew up. I was raised in a small, conservative town with family values, but now I was out exploring the world. I left the comfortable conservative climate for an opposing one. I don't think I realized the differences till I was surrounded by people that thought differently than me. People seemed darker and angry about everything, politics, religion, you name it. Protests for some kind of injustice were normal. There seemed to be a negative cloud over the people that never really left. Over time, this critical atmosphere began to influence my perspective and shape my worldview.

The environment seemed to press against my belief system and challenge what I knew about myself and God. I had the question looming ahead of me. *What kind of person am I going to be?* Am I a product of my upbringing or am I to change into something else entirely? Being raised Christian I knew that there are sides to this world, a light and a dark, a good and an evil. That concept had always been easy for me to understand and feel around me. There is a war for mankind and what we can potentially be. What I didn't realize is that participating in that war is unavoidable. You have to choose a side.

Chained

Later I found myself in my dorm room in the heart of the city surrounded by darkness. I must admit that I was not walking in purity in that season. I sinned against God and myself. I was raised a Christian yet I still had unrelenting chains that kept me from ever taking off. As I sat with the lights off I contemplated my condition. Guilt and shame were on the edge of my ears taunting me, but the Lord began to minister to me and He asked me about the people around my vicinity.

Just outside I could see people using illegal drugs. In the room to my right was a homosexual couple and to my left was a couple that was sleeping around. The building next door was a transgender community that was hard to ignore. I was surrounded by different people all engaged in different lifestyles that were contrary to what I believed was morally right.

Everyone needs to be saved. We all need Jesus to step into our situations and remind us of who we really are and to actually set us free. My neighbors didn't need theology, or debates, they needed the power of God's love. I never thought I would be in this position where I could not help them because I wasn't any freer than they were from sin. I wasn't any better than any other person around me and it was painfully obvious. I might believe that my religious faith and disposition might grant me more slack than those around me but I was wrong. My sinful tendencies were just different from others. We are all a work in progress.

I found myself wanting to do the right thing but I couldn't. My lifestyle was riddled with wrong choices that hurt me and others around me. It was hard to accept that I was a prisoner to sin, and it had an unrelenting hold on me. Even if I could elicit enough self-control and discipline to avoid a destructive action my resistance to it wouldn't last long. The fight often left me weary and the enemy constantly tried to convince me that giving up and giving in is easier. No matter how hard I tried I could not set myself free. I lacked the endurance it was going to take to go the distance.

When I choose to give into sin I'm reinforcing its hold on me. Sin is like an arrow that an archer shoots at a target and then the arrow misses the mark.

It's falling short of the standard that was laid out by the Creator. The rules of what is morally right and wrong are not arbitrary. They are not simply rules to some cruel game that we all lose at. The standard does not change regardless of what is politically correct or accepted by people. His nature is the standard, and His nature doesn't change. We don't set the rules of morality but we do live in them. Most people would agree that murder is morally wrong but to accept that standard you have to answer where that standard came from. God's nature is the standard of right and anything that deviates from His character reveals whats wrong.

The Prison

This enemy which is one or even multiple evil spirits (see Ephesians 6:12), is not interested in giving you a good time or making your dreams come true; their agenda is to kill, steal, and destroy you (see John 10:10). They first tempt you with something, making you feel like you want to do the thing you don't want to do. When you agree with that feeling and act on it, the enemy associated with it then betrays you with accusation and guilt for giving in to the very thing with which they tempted you. They are wicked and can never be trusted! They attack your identity and tear you down. They want to keep you focused on a perceived weakness, because if they keep you distracted looking at yourself then you won't ever look at Jesus and discover who you truly are.

A sign of being trapped in sin is it has a repetitive nature to it. One tactic is they let you think you're in control and you can stop anytime you want. They can even let you feel confident and in charge, but the moment you start taking flight into who you're called to be they yank on that chain and pull you down. It's called slavery. At that point, the prison guards, named guilt and shame, follow up with lies to keep you under control and to keep you quiet.

Guilt makes you feel bad for something you actually did. It gives you no hope of escape. Shame tries to convince you into thinking you are that thing and you will never change. Shame is tricky because it targets your identity. It says you are your sin. One guard pulls you down, the other takes your wallet and substitutes it for a pile of garbage then tells you that you are that garbage.

If you believe the lie then you will never be free. You're not supposed to be a prisoner, you're supposed to live in a palace ruling like God originally intended. *(see Romans 8:17).*

Our lives are shaped by what we believe. It's not the sin that traps you, it's the lie that you are your sin that keeps you from discovering the truth. You were born for freedom and believing the lie gives us an excuse to live as less than we were created to be.

I thought I had avoided picking a side but I found myself at a crossroads. I needed to decide what I believed. I couldn't handle the arguments in my mind any longer. I was sick and tired of the guilt and shame from poor decisions. Somewhere on this journey, I wandered away. One way or the other you decide by the choices you make what kind of person you're going to be. You decide how much dark you partake in. You also decide how much light you reject.

One Single Second

After I worshiped a bit I had a conversation with the Holy Spirit. We had to settle things once and for all. *(see Isaiah 1:18)* I knew that moment was a defining moment and that I would be responsible for what I heard.

I asked the Lord, "Can I live without sin? Is it even possible?" I waited a moment and the Holy Spirit spoke right into me, "**With Me you can. Do you have faith to live without sin for 1 second?**" His words echoed inside my heart and at that moment faith came and unlocked me. I wiped a tear away and said to myself surely I have faith for one second.

My inner processing continued and I had to answer a fundamental question. Did Jesus' death on the cross pay the price for my sin or not? If I am claiming to believe the truth but I am not free, then do I really believe it is true? Or am I just tricking myself so I feel a bit better about my guilt?

We need to stop pretending and decide whether we believe in the power of the cross or not. What we believe about what God did for us shapes everything. What we refuse to believe keeps us bound while the truth God gives sets us free.

Righteous Power

"God sent us His Son in human form to identify with human weakness. Clothed with humanity, God's Son gave His body to be the sin-offering so that God could once and for all condemn the guilt and power of sin. So now every righteous requirement of the law can be fulfilled through the Anointed One living His life in us. And we are free to live, not according to our flesh, but by the dynamic power of the Holy Spirit!" Romans 8:3-4 (TPT)

The law reveals our sin and requires just payment. On the cross, Jesus became sin for us and nailed the list of all our sins to Himself as us. In this, He fulfilled the righteous requirement of the law. *"For God made the only one who did not know sin to become sin for us, so that we who did not know righteousness might become the righteousness of God through our union with Him." 2 Corinthians 5:21 (TPT)*

In the same motion as Jesus rose from the dead He declares us righteous. Jesus was handed over to be crucified for the forgiveness of our sins and was raised back to life to prove that He had made us right with God! *(see Romans 4:25)* He declared us righteous which means to be right with God. I'm not righteous because I never make a mistake. I'm righteous because He said so, and because I believe Him.

When you repent and yield to the Holy Spirit in your life there is power available that's stronger than any temptation or sin. Some things that we need to let go of change instantly, and some things take time, but the Lord is always in each breakthrough. As a believer, we still live in a world rampant with darkness and sin. Sometimes things stick to us and sometimes we make a choice of living less than we are created to be. As a believer when we give into temptation we sin by faith. The difference is we have an advocate who is Jesus Himself who pleads our case before the Father. *(see 1 John 2:1)* The Father sees the blood that Jesus paid and declares us not guilty. Even in those moments when your mind, heart, or body are committing a sin, it doesn't change what He says about you. You can't change His mind, trying to prove it is like saying the blood of Jesus isn't good enough for you. A lifestyle of sinning stops when you have a revelation of His love that is stronger than your revelation about how bad you are.

Another beautiful key to living without sin can be found in 1 John 2:1(NIV) which says *"My dear children, I write this to you so that you will not sin."* Which reveals to us that it must be possible to live without it. Before Christ, we are a slave to our sins but after Christ, we are free from sin. He continually cleanses us from sin by His blood. Jesus steps into our place and presents the finishing remarks by simply presenting His own scars as evidence of the reality of where you stand with Him. Accepted

Something rose up in me that day in college and I decided that even if I am the only person in my dorm that believes in Jesus and the freedom He paid for then so be it. The choice was mine alone and I knew too much to turn back. Freedom from sin is already available so I'm going to fight for the evidence in my life. I refuse to back down until I get what He paid for. If I have to wait until I die to be free from sin, then that would make death my savior, not Jesus.

God isn't afraid of your sin. It was His plan the whole time to get rid of it and wipe you clean long before you even chose Him. He imparts to you a greater power through His Holy Spirit that frees you from the power of sin. *(see Romans 8:1)* So now you no longer have to live with your mistakes pulling you down but you can live free by the grace of God which He freely gives to you.

Become Something New

After we come to understand and begin to believe what Jesus did for us on the cross we can leave behind the old and become something new.

"Therefore, if anyone is in Christ, he is a new creation; old things have passed away; behold, all things have become new." 2 Corinthians 5:17 (NKJV)

The word "creation" in this verse means prototype. This means you are a new original model in which there has never been anything like you before. We no longer view our life through the old lens of an old man that has died, but we view our lives through God's compassionate eyes. What He sees is actually who you really are. Holy and blameless.

"Yet now he has reconciled you to Himself through the death of Christ in his physical body. As a result, he has brought you into his own presence, and you are holy and blameless as you stand before Him without a single fault". Colossians 1:22 (NLT)

Staying Free

If Jesus' sacrifice could not set me free from sin then there was no point in Him dying. He might as well show up at the point of salvation and take people to glory. But instead, He lets us live life with Him on a beautiful discovery. You are a demonstration of God's immeasurable love for all of heaven to watch and every invisible thing to bear witness. Jesus proved by the way He lived that you can live without sin when you live in Him. The first reason Jesus came as a man was to demonstrate how God the Father truly feels about people. The second reason was to restore our relationship with God by paying for our sins. The third reason He came was to demonstrate what fully yielding to the Holy Spirit looks like.

The Mind

Freedom is found when you truly know who you are in Christ. It is maintained through the power of the Holy Spirit and understanding the reality of who you are in Him. The greatest obstacle to the journey is found in our minds. Every battle is won or lost first in our minds, and this is the place we need to re calibrate.

What we think about ourselves matters. We can't afford to have thoughts about ourselves that Jesus isn't having about us. If it doesn't line up with what He thinks about us then I refuse to entertain it. If I do, then I risk believing a lie. Lies are shackles designed to destroy you. In the words of Paul, *"This is no afternoon athletic contest that we'll walk away from and forget about in a couple of hours. This is for keeps, a life-or-death fight to the finish against the Devil and all his angels." Ephesians 6:10-12 (MSG)* Your thought life either attracts the kingdom of heaven or the kingdom of darkness. Cultivate a thought life that is full of goodness and stay away from hopeless ways of thinking. You become what you think about yourself. If a thought isn't in the heart of God, cast it down and refuse to give it any power in your life. That's why it's important to be influenced by Jesus instead of whatever wandering spirit walks by. We will talk more about this later.

Identity

"It is no longer I that live, but Christ lives in me." Galatians 2:20 (NLT)

Your old nature is dead and buried. Unhealthy choices are no longer your nature. You're a new creation and that means you don't make a practice of sin, but instead you focus on righteous living. Your identity is built on who God says you are. In Christ you are His, you are holy, blameless, righteous, forgiven, complete, free, called, chosen, loved, trusted, seated with Him in heavenly places, hidden in Him, just to name a few. There is a lifetime of discovering the different facets of God and how they are available to you.

When you're a believer, sin takes on a different meaning. It's still missing the mark but it's more like you choosing to live less than He created you to be. Instead of shame and guilt which are trying to trap you, you receive conviction from the Holy Spirit who is calling you upwards into fellowship with Jesus and His Father. There is still repentance but the focus is different. Your motivation is not based on not doing the wrong thing... it's more about how your choice affects Him and your relationship. The relationship is the very reason you were born. It's the reason Jesus came to prove to you how wide, how long, how high, and how deep His love is. *(see Ephesians 3:18)* Jesus came from His glorious heaven to the lowest and darkest parts of the earth to find you. He paid for all the wrong things you have ever done and anything you might ever do. When you build on Jesus the enemy can't tear it down because they can't kill what is eternal. We are judged not by the darkness we partake in but by the light that we reject. *(see John 3:19)*

Encounter Grace

We can learn all the scriptures and pray all the prayers and still be controlled by our impulses. We have to encounter His presence and receive an impartation of His grace. *"For by grace you have been saved through faith, and that not of yourselves; it is the gift of God."* *Ephesians 2:8 (NKJV)*

When I believed the truth about who I am in Christ I received grace. Grace is the enabling ability to do something you could not do before. It is the power to do the right thing, to keep a clean mind and therefore a clean heart. It's the manifested reality of faith. By grace, through faith, you are aligning with God's truth about you. The shackles unlocked and I was given the faith that I can live without sin for one second! I then realized that means I can live for two. If I can live for two seconds then I can live for a minute. At that point, the argument was all over because faith grows stronger the longer it lives. *(See Romans 4:20)*

My conversation with the Lord on that day gave me the faith to live righteously for a single second. It was a tiny glimpse of what was possible with Jesus, which is anything. I made a promise to Jesus that day that if He freed me from sin then I would serve Him forever. He keeps His promises and I keep mine. Many of my chains I haven't seen in years, and when I find some He crushes them into oblivion. He is in the business of rewriting our past and impacting our future.

Practice Freedom

When you have your mind focused on Jesus and who He says you are, you have His grace to do what you could not do before. You will be in a position to live free in a particular area for the rest of your life. Start by practicing. Track small victories and write them down so you can be reminded. One of the most basic strategies for living without sin is perseverance. Not the kind of thing where you try with all your might. The kind of perseverance where you let God fight for you and you refuse to move to any sound that is not His voice. The enemy does not have as much perseverance as you have, because you have the

Holy Spirit and He is eternal. Your well of potential comes from the eternal source. You can hold your stance with the Lord and the enemy will give up. It may be very hard to stand, but the more victories you have the more the enemy will believe that you are serious, when you say no.

The Wager

In the new testament Jesus said to a woman that was caught in the act of adultery. *"Go and sin no more" John 8:11 (NKJV)* Jesus is not like us. He can not lie. So He must believe people could actually live without sin. Do you? There is a wager in heaven that Jesus can actually change the heart of a person. Jesus bet everything on you. He believes you can live completely free, and as a result be truly alive. He's confident in His Father and He's confident in who you are becoming. Something completely new.

"The spirit of God lives in you." Romans 8:10 (Paraphrase)

"For this is how God loved the world: He gave his one and only Son, so that everyone who believes in Him will not perish but have eternal life. God sent his Son into the world not to judge the world, but to save the world through Him. "There is no judgment against anyone who believes in Him. But anyone who does not believe in Him has already been judged for not believing in God's one and only Son. And the judgment is based on this fact: God's light came into the world, but people loved the darkness more than the light, for their actions were evil." John 3:16-19 (NLT)

"When Jesus had raised Himself up and saw no one but the woman, He said to her, 'Woman, where are those accusers of yours? Has no one condemned you?'She said, 'No one, Lord.' And Jesus said to her, 'Neither do I condemn you; go and sin no more'" John 8:10-11 (NKJV)

5

The Mountain

"Afterward Jesus went up on a mountain and called out the ones he wanted to go with Him. And they came to Him." Mark 3:13 (NLT)

Sunday Morning

On June 4th, 2006 which was Pentecost Sunday I was sitting in my chair. The service was nearing the end and it was a special Sunday because people were lining up to get baptized. I love seeing people declare their faith in God and their desire to know God more. It always stirs me because there is something special about a person declaring their commitment to Christ and an opportunity to hear why. It reminds the viewers of their own promises and it challenges us to bring things back to the simplicity of the cross. One by one people would get in the tub, say a few words and down they went into the water. They would come out a different person.

Jesus had His own baptism experience.

"Then Jesus left Galilee to come to the Jordan river to be baptized by John. But when he waded into the water, John resisted Him, saying, "Why are you doing this? I'm the one who needs to be baptized by you, and yet you come to be baptized

by me?" Jesus replied, "It is only right to do all that God requires." Then John baptized Jesus. And as Jesus rose up out of the water, the heavenly realm opened up over Him and he saw the Holy Spirit descend out of the heavens and rest upon Him in the form of a dove. Then suddenly the voice of the Father shouted from the sky, saying, "This is the Son I love, and my greatest delight is in Him." Matthew 3:13-17 (TPT)

Jesus' baptism is leading by example and putting others ahead of Himself. He saw the value of what baptism would mean for humanity. Baptism is a declaration of where your loyalty lies. Heaven and earth witness your declaration. Baptism in water and by the Holy Spirit is essential to living out an effective relationship with God.

My pastor had finished with those that signed up and offered one last time to the congregation, "Anyone else want to be baptized?" I was a little scared but I knew it was time. I felt the Lord calling me to step up not for anyone else but for Him. I knew He called me, I knew there was more, and it was my choice to respond. I waited for years under the disguise of not knowing enough, or not fully understanding what baptism was, however I didn't really pursue the answers to my excuses. This particular morning I had an urgency in me to obey and to do it quickly, to move before my opportunity was gone. I stood up and went forward. I embraced the discomfort and chose to take a different path up the mountain that I had previously ignored. I knew it was significant and I knew there was no turning back.

Responding to God

Moses had a specific time with God where He had the choice to respond to the Lord or to ignore His calling.

"Now Moses was tending the flock of Jethro, his father-in-law, the priest of Midian. And he led the flock to the back of the desert, and came to Horeb, the mountain of God. And the Angel of the LORD appeared to Him in a flame of fire from the midst of a bush. So he looked, and behold, the bush was burning with fire, but the bush was not consumed. Then Moses said, "I will now turn aside and see this great sight, why the bush does not burn." So when the LORD saw that he

turned aside to look, God called to Him from the midst of the bush and said, "Moses, Moses!" And he said, "Here I am."" Exodus 3:1-4 (NKJV)

Notice Moses said *"I will now turn aside and see this great sight."* Moses had to turn away from His daily work, his plan, His responsibilities to discover the destiny God had planned long before Moses was even born. Can you imagine if Moses never turned aside from His path to investigate the burning bush? Our world could have been very different if Moses didn't respond. Thankfully He did.

How many metaphorical burning bushes has God put on our paths that we didn't take the time to turn aside? If we responded would we have walked into our purpose, or walked into the answers we have been praying for? I propose the Lord places burning bushes on our path more than we know. They are invitations to opportunities that propel us on our journey and all we need to do is turn aside and engage with the Lord.

The Mountain

I see a mountain in my mind that represents our life in God and all the paths we can walk on this journey to climb to the top. The top of this mountain represents the place where we are transformed by His presence, when we truly know Him, and when we become like Him. The slope of the mountain represents the difficulty. The path we take represents our journey. How long we take to get to the top is dependent on our surrender and obedience to His leading. He's the only one that knows the way.

As we are on this journey we are going to see paths that ascend and descend. We're going to travel paths that are rockier than others. Some are more beautiful and peaceful than others. They are all important parts of the journey with God we call our life. There are times on this journey when we come to a crossroads, that point when we have to decide where we're going to go. Sometimes we can see where the path goes, sometimes we can't. I believe there are times when the crossroad is a place that we have actually been before. Have you ever found yourself at the same place having to make the same decision you made months and even years earlier? You might have looked up and saw a sign that reads "Are you ready to surrender more?" Some things in life we push off for another convenient day and we choose to keep walking around the mountain. We do that for lots of reasons: fear, unbelief, love of something else, comfort, money, selfishness, etc. All of these reasons delay what God has for our lives. Sometimes that invitation when we get the choice again takes a long time to come around the mountain, but when it does we recognize it.

God is very kind because He waits for us. He'll continue to walk around that mountain with us and meet us where we are at. But He longs for us to leave our limitations behind and ascend higher on the mountain where we can experience a greater intimacy with Him. He longs for us to fulfill what we were made for; to live free, full of grace and completely aware of His love for us.

When that moment at the crossroads comes and He asks us for something, He gives us something in return...His presence. The relationship isn't about God taking things from us and trying to control us, it's about choosing freedom from things that hold us back. He is concerned about anything that limits us. The surrender God is looking for isn't about rules, it's about enabling us to rise above our present circumstances and fulfilling all that we were made to be. His dreams for us are bigger than ours.

Baptism Crossroad

Getting baptized in water at church was a difficult crossroad for me. I was afraid of what other people would think. I was raised in a Christian environment but never water baptized. It was something that wasn't emphasized in my early years, but when I was older, it was more common. People got saved on a Sunday morning then they were baptized, that was the culture. Because the Lord had been in my life since as long as I could remember I felt like I must have missed my chance when I was younger. I believed the lie and I disqualified myself before I even started.

I will admit that the invitation the Holy Spirit gave me on this day, I have had before. I didn't respond previously but I knew it was time to pick up my cross and carry it to the baptismal tank. It was time to put this thing to death once and for all, so that I could truly live. The signpost on this crossroad was clear, it just required obedience. It was not an issue of whether baptism was required or not, but a question of: if God has it for you... why not take a hold of it? What's keeping us from climbing?

Buried in Baptism

Baptism, which can be seen as an old tradition, has a spiritual significance that the apostle Paul talks about in *Romans 6:2-4 (TPT) "We have died to sin once and for all, as a dead man passes away from this life. So how could we live under sin's rule a moment longer? Or have you forgotten that all of us who were immersed into union with Jesus, the Anointed One, were immersed into union with his death? Sharing in his death by our baptism means that we were co-buried and entombed with Him, so that when the Father's glory raised Christ from the dead, we were also raised with Him. We have been co-resurrected with Him so that we could be empowered to walk in the freshness of new life."*

Baptism in water is a physical demonstration and a prophetic act of burying our old nature in the accomplished work of Jesus. As we go down into the water the Lord cuts away all the old things that are contrary to Him and as we come out of the water we are stepping into a Spirit filled life with a changed heart. This whole time I thought I was supposed to deny my sin nature but the reality is once I was saved, my old man was buried in the baptismal tank.

As scripture reads in *Romans 6:4 (NLT) "For we died and were buried with Christ by baptism. And just as Christ was raised from the dead by the glorious power of the Father, now we also may live new lives."* Verse 8 *"since we died with Christ, we know we will also live with Him."*

Baptism reflects the inner work of the cross and creates a landing pad for the Spirit of God to encounter us. When we come out of the water we are coming into His resurrection life. It is an invitation to live in the Spirit and to pursue a life of knowing Jesus.

Climbing

Around the same time that I was baptized I was still in school in San Francisco. I felt the Lord drawing me to the mountain to spend time with Him. Sometimes the day would end and I would feel as if I didn't accomplish why I lived that day. It was a burning that only subsided when I responded to His heart. There was something quiet about the whole world being asleep while I stood and watched for the Holy Spirit to come. I had a singular focus of pursuing His presence and all I wanted to do was stay there. Some things we only discover when we take the time to value what matters. We attract what we honor.

A great example of this is in the life of Jesus Himself. *"And when He had sent the multitudes away, He went up on the mountain by Himself to pray. Now when evening came, He was alone there."* Matthew 14:23 (NKJV)

Jesus climbed a mountain to pursue His Father constantly. He would step away from the crowds and responsibilities He had, and set His attention on His relationship with God. He valued His Father and prioritized Him. The miracles that followed Him were a byproduct of that relationship.

Prioritizing Prayer

Often I'd climb to the top of Nob Hill in downtown San Francisco and I'd walk around Grace Cathedral, just looking for Jesus and touching His presence. I spent a lot of time in prayer connecting to the Holy Spirit and getting to know Him. One of the best ways to climb is to pray. Go deeper to climb higher. That's where we find fresh water, that's where we find His presence, and most importantly we find Him. I'd embrace the quietest moments of the city and we would just talk.

What We Find on the Mountain

Climbing the mountain is a prophetic picture of our walk with God. Height takes time and costs us more, but at each crossroad we make a decision of the kind of person we're going to be. When we climb the mountain in pursuit of knowing Jesus, we find Him. *"In those days when you pray, I will listen. If you look for me wholeheartedly, you will find me." Jeremiah 29:12-13. (NLT)*

Realize it's not about religion or performance at all. It's not about rules of what to do and not to do. It's about a relationship with God who gave everything just so we would have the option to get to know Him. It's not about believing the truth, it's knowing the truth that matters. We have to know Him or we have nothing, and that takes intentional time with Him.

When we climb the mountain we lean into God. He pours His presence upon us and we begin to change. Some hindrances fall off right away and other obstacles take time but we begin to transform into something we have never seen before but we know it's who we are created to be. When we lean into His presence the part of our heart that's empty and longs for significance gets filled. In God's presence we partake of His divine nature as He lives in us.

"By his divine power, God has given us everything we need for living a godly life. We have received all of this by coming to know Him, the one who called us to Himself by means of his marvelous glory and excellence. And because of his glory and excellence, he has given us great and precious promises. These are the promises that enable you to share his divine nature and escape the world's corruption caused by human desires." 2 Peter 1:3-4 (NLT)

Transforming

"Let God transform you into a new person by changing the way you think. Then you will learn to know God's will for you, which is good and pleasing and perfect." Romans 12:2 (NLT)

When we encounter His presence and partake of His divine nature it changes us. Our mind sharpens and we think His thoughts. We come into alignment and we think with the mind of Christ concerning our life. (see *1 Cor 2:16*)

Jesus said in *John 5:39 (NLT) "You are busy analyzing the Scriptures, frantically poring over them in hopes of gaining eternal life. Everything you read points to me."* That would mean the stories of Moses, Joseph, Daniel, David, Isaiah all point to Jesus, just to name a few.

Renewing the mind is often thought of as meditating on the word. The truth is Jesus is the Word. So encountering Him IS the renewing of the mind. It's in that place when we connect to Him, where we actually learn what He thinks about us and we truly transform not by our mind but by His presence.

Purpose

When we discover His divine nature manifested by the presence of the Holy Spirit we find our purpose for life and our calling. We were created by God to be loved by Him. Our highest purpose is to know Him and our calling is to carry His presence to the world.

I would like to propose that there is more of His presence available today than ever before. Moses lived face to face with God as a friend even though He wasn't full of the spirit. How much more friendship should we live in when we have His presence in us? How can an older covenant have a greater manifestation of Him than the new covenant we live in? It sure shouldn't. We need to raise the bar of what we can expect God to do in us and through us.

Success is not measured by how much money we make, or how many friends we have, but by moments where we can touch His glory and step into who we are created to be. For me it took hours of prayer and worship to have just a momentary touch of His presence. In time when I learned to strive less and use faith more, it became easier to connect. My heart had to be changed and my mind needed to transform to protect when His presence came. It's not about the amount of time, it's about deciding that you're not moving your heart until He connects to it. Practice connecting and recognizing when He walks into the room.

The Source

We need to be people that are so single focused that we go get answers right from the source. We need to be the kind of people that recognize the call of God inviting us to climb the mountain into a deeper relationship with Him. We courageously ascend the fiery mountain bent on one thing: just to know

Him and see what He has on His heart for today. We might just find what we have been looking for this whole time.

God has things to show us that He has never shown anyone. There are inventions that He is waiting to give to someone who is willing. There is power available to those who would carry it. There is an immeasurable amount of His presence for us to live in. We just have to dive in and leave the old behind. Take hold of the new and begin to climb the mountain. If you knew that God has more for you... would you want it?

Dream Crossroad

I had a crossroad that came in the form of a dream. I had a split decision to make and the consequences mattered. I was sleeping in my dorm room and in my dream I saw myself, although I was much older. My face was full of light. My skin and hair were glowing and I had the biggest smile. I gleamed with the presence of the Holy Spirit, and I had such joy. Then the dream changed and I saw myself in darkness. My face was tired, and my eyes were dark. My skin was pale and my life was a result of living in sin without God. With both choices faded away I heard a booming voice echo deep inside me. *"Choose this very day, who you will serve."* I woke up shaking with the presence of the Holy Spirit on my body, I was on fire from head to toe laying in my bed. I spoke out loud in my room. I said "Lord, You know everything there is about me. You know my choice. I choose you and I always will." I knew He heard me and that day is marked a day I chose His path up the mountain. I knew that God called me to know Him and to represent Him.

"I knew you before I formed you in your mother's womb. Before you were born I set you apart and appointed you as my prophet to the nations... Go wherever I send you and say whatever I tell you." Jeremiah 1:5-7 (NLT)

I spent years taking the wrong road. Even in art college my days were full of hours of quiet solitude but while I was there, Jesus would meet with me. He gave me His presence, value and purpose. He gave me a voice and required that I use it to share what He's saying. We climb up the mountain to be with

Him, and we climb down to demonstrate Him to the world. Everyone is faced with their own unique crossroad moments, when you are given the choice to turn aside and engage the Lord. What will you do?

"Who may climb the mountain of the Lord? Who may stand in his holy place? Only those whose hands and hearts are pure, who do not worship idols and never tell lies. They will receive the Lord's blessing and have a right relationship with God, their savior. Such people may seek you and worship in your presence, O God of Jacob." Psalm 24:3-6 (NLT)

"I admit that I haven't yet acquired the absolute fullness that I'm pursuing, but I run with passion into his abundance so that I may reach the purpose that Jesus Christ has called me to fulfill and wants me to discover. I don't depend on my own strength to accomplish this; however, I do have one compelling focus: I forget all of the past as I fasten my heart to the future instead. I run straight for the divine invitation of reaching the heavenly goal and gaining the victory-prize through the anointing of Jesus." Philippians 3:12-14 (TPT)

6

Hunger

"Blessed are those who hunger and thirst for righteousness, for they shall be filled."
Matt 5:6 (NKJV)

Over the Ocean

The dark city had been home long enough. I wasn't just craving change. I was hungry to encounter God on a deeper level. I grew up with Christian traditions that were expressed mostly out of honor. I had been surrounded by ankle-deep Christianity my whole life and I needed more then a fun Sunday school idea. The desire alone was not enough to satisfy. I needed to know the Holy Spirit in new ways if that was even possible. Leaving everything behind that had been normal, I went to a Bible school in the United Kingdom which seamed to be the perfect setup where transformation felt inevitable.

Back in San Francisco there were moments with God's presence but I wanted to know Him on a deeper measure and had a feeling He did too. The call on my life was undeniable and I was ready to do something about it.

Bible school became a crucible that demanded everything. The presence of God wasn't just talked about but experienced daily. The teaching was rich and spirit-led, like a drink of water after years in a desert. Living in Christ alone was the focus, and the Holy Spirit brought truth like a hammer, breaking down everything that stood in His way.

As the soil of my heart was turned over, I saw how overgrown it had become. Weeds I once ignored were suddenly front and center. Weaknesses I once dismissed now demanded to be addressed. The deeper work had begun

Time for Change

Surrender wasn't a one-time prayer, it was a deliberate, daily offering. Prayer became the rhythm, Scripture the anchor. Fasting became more than abstaining, it was alignment with God's heart. The journey with the Holy Spirit became a constant pursuit. When He felt near, there was peace. When He felt far, fear and insecurity tried to creep in.

Fasting sharpened sensitivity to His presence. Quieting my body allowed my Spirit to lead the way, just as it was meant to. My hunger for God only deepened, until living outside His presence was no longer an option.

Still, fear lingered. What if I miss Him? What if I fail again? With every familiar comfort stripped away; family, friends, culture norms, food, entertainment there was nowhere to hide. The raw truth was evident and it was time to face what had long been avoided. There was only one option: to hold fast to the Lord, to stare fear in the face, and to demand its surrender. The time for change had come.

Weeds

As a result of pursuing Jesus He has a way of uprooting dark areas of our hearts. He reveals places where weeds have been growing so deep you didn't even realize they were there. He sees you past all the weeds and begins a good work in cleaning the garden of your heart so you can grow something beautiful. Jesus began to hollow me out and heal me in a way that only He could do.

I grew up as the middle child in a blended family of five. We had his, hers, and ours. I was the firstborn of "ours," yet I never saw myself that way. From the beginning, I was raised to believe I was the middle child, in hopes of helping my older half-brothers feel fully accepted. And while they were embraced as part of the family, the effort to mend past broken relationships unintentionally diminished my own sense of worth. Over time, the Lord revealed that I had never truly recognized my rightful position and not just in my family, but also in Christ.

Born into a family with broken relationships positioned me to be the peacemaker. Divorce produces void spaces in us that we try to fill. It's hard to fix something that was never meant to break. Seeing the pain in both directions trained me very quickly to perform a specific way and stay out of the conflict. I felt like my other siblings needed more attention than me, and my parents seemed to reinforce my observations. With attention absent, even learning to ride a bike or swim became a solo journey of trial and error, guided only by the Holy Spirit.

Because of my turbulent family and my non-confrontational nature I learned to sacrifice for the sake of others. I accepted a lie that I wasn't valuable enough to have attention and my environment, upbringing, and unhealthy thinking reinforced it. I resigned myself to the back seat so others could go ahead of me.

Sacrifice is valuable when it costs you something you're willing to give. It's self destructive if the sacrifice is done with depreciation of your value. Feeling like an inconvenience led to a deep fear of rejection, and failure. Fear motivated me to be "Perfect." With a perfect performance then maybe that would somehow earn me the love and acceptance my heart desperately wanted.

That same mindset unintentionally followed into Bible school like a form of baggage that slowed my climb up the mountain. I took everything that made me unique and crucified it for the sake of being perfect. Individuality was dismantled under the guise of sacrifice. While my sinful tendencies demanded attention.

I wanted to be different than I was, something better but what would I have to do to have it. Was attending biblically based education going to do the work? What was it going to cost me... and was I willing to pay it. I needed to move from faith to tangible Holy Spirit power so I could actually live on the tier that is required.

Hunger

I've spent the first few chapters of this book in the perspective of **faith** and lessons I learned along the way. But now we're shifting into something different. These next few chapters focus more on anointing. Faith is more about believing something that you have no evidence of. Which is a powerful thing and is essential to our journey. However there is another level where you actually experience His presence not the theory the actual manifestation that affects your spirit, soul and body. We need to come into an alignment with Him in such a way that the outpouring of our life is a manifestation of a higher kingdom. That manifestation is His anointing which flows right from the King.

Before we dive in, I need to be honest with you. Really honest. I can't talk about breakthrough without first talking about the battle. This section is intentionally raw because I want you to *feel* what I walked through. Not the highlight reel... just the real.

I didn't have everything figured out then. I still don't. But maybe you'll see yourself in these words... and just maybe my breakthrough can become yours too.

After a month in Bible school, I was still wrestling with the same insecurities, the same toxic thought patterns, and of course the same addictions. I thought a new place would change me. It didn't. Those tendencies just followed me across oceans.

So let me ask you:

What are you willing to do to truly be transformed?

What are you willing to do to hold on to Jesus as you voyage through the unknown?

In Genesis 32 Jacob wrestled with an angel all night. The angel couldn't get free until he dislocated Jacob's hip, and Jacob couldn't get free till the angel would bless Him. He was done being who he had been. What does your wrestling look like?

The Wrestle

In art school I had classical education that included drawing the human body. One of the skills learned was to see through clothing and be able to draw human form. It was a kind of X-ray vision that I automatically did when I saw people, and I was good at it. However lust and shame took advantage of it and it massively affected my purity. I conditioned my mind in such a way that it was hard to look at people. It wasn't that I lusted after everyone, I didn't. But it became difficult to focus on the right things when there were alarms going off.

How does a man live pure in our world where everything is sexualized? Almost everywhere you go there is something that is designed to draw you in. I tried to resist, but that only seemed to make things harder. I was addicted to self pleasure, food, caffeine, sugar, anything that filled my soul wounds tied to my lack of identity and self-worth.

On any given day, my wrestle looked something like this:

I was staying in a small room in an English home. Through the wall, I could hear the neighbor's arguing through the wall. I got up, put in my headphones, and played worship music. I felt spiritually dry and that I needed His water. I listened until I felt His peace on my chest. It took a few songs but He was there. I went back to bed.

When I wake up I feel cold, spiritually numb, physically weak and hungry for more than just food. I have been fasting for at least a few weeks now and who knows how long this will go. I'm still the same so I won't stop. I can't stop.

Back into prayer I focus on letting go of the shame attached to the nightmares I had. Were the nightmares mine or were they my neighbors? I'll figure that out one day.

Get ready, get going. Standing up is slow. Can't move too fast or you'll be light headed. I notice a cut on my hand hasn't healed. Apparently your body doesn't regenerate when you don't give it food. Looking in the mirror I notice my eyes have turned yellow. I hope that is reversible. My body has sores in various places not because of being unclean but because your body relies on the nutrients to regenerate. Didn't know that before. Don't care that much, can't turn back now.

Take the walk up the hill to class slowly, to keep any damage to a minimum. Rain the whole way. Not really present to see the beauty of the place I live. Keep your eyes on Jesus. Stay in His presence.

We started class with an hour of prayer time which at first seems like forever, but in reality is just the warm up for what the day is really going to need. I participate but I don't feel worthy to contribute, so I keep my mouth shut. What you have to share can't be accurate. It can't have value because you don't value yourself. Old lies are still holding me. You still had an unclean thought before you walked into the room. Am I worthy? Better luck next time.

He says that I am… so I press in. If I do then I won't feel human. I won't feel my weaknesses demanding my submission. I'll submit to Christ instead. We are learning about being In Christ Alone. Does that mean none of me? How do I get rid of everything that is not in Christ…not a big deal, I don't like me anyways.

The message is encouraging and I hope it sticks. When class ends I trek down the hill but I don't go home. Going home felt dangerous, I don't want the spiritual fight today. It's better to stay around people, but not too close. A coffee shop will do. Do you feel His peace…. It's still there. Ok… you're all right. Play some music and be intentional. Get it in you. Get the truth in you.

Get my Bible out and read. Read it all. Gotta find Jesus. Gotta find my bread for today. Will yesterday's bread work… just a little… ok keep eating keep looking you might need something later. Get the word…. Read it and read it. It has to be enough. Absorb. Take in the Spirit… He is stirring.. focus…I sense Him in me and on me. I feel complete.

Drink in. Drink it. Suddenly feeling thirsty and tired so I get another coffee. The cafe is closing so it's back into the rain. There is an old church nearby. It's quiet there, maybe He will talk to you there. Carry His presence with you.

You wait in the door a moment to make sure He is still there. Yep. We're good to go.

Walking to the English church, it's maybe a few hundred years old, the kind where it is surrounded by gravestones. All these people are dead, did they ever really live? Did they have the freedom I'm looking for? Does anyone? Whatever it takes...I'm still here so God must have a plan for me. Ignore the feeling of insecurity and remember He chose me so I have to keep going. Music on.. reconnect. The song isn't working. Try a different song.. repeat. I have a 45 minute walk home to prepare for what might be waiting for me there. Pray all the way and stay in His presence. Keep going. Abide.

When I get home I skip dinner. Food has ruled me before. Now I rule it. I won't respond to its voice. I want God's presence more than I want food, because only His presence has the power to truly change me.

Climb into my sleeping bag and prepare for the cold. Laying on my back I reach out looking for Jesus. Do you feel Him?... He's still there. Ok... you're all right. He is still with you. I tried my best, was it enough, will abiding tomorrow be easier? His presence kisses me on the forehead. I fell asleep knowing I did everything I could, but was it enough? I feel love.

A few hours later I woke up and I felt war going on. Time to get up. Music on....I stand in the center of the room until His presence returns. Connection only took 2 songs this time. I remain there and grab hold of Jesus. There is somewhere we need to go in the spirit. I'm available. I have to be. This road to connection needs to be shorter. I need to get good at abiding. Keep trying. Stay connected. Sleep before dawn.

What is the Point?

I share this not to glorify struggle but to show the honest, gritty side of walking with God when everything in you feels broken. It wasn't neat. It wasn't pretty. It wasn't always victorious. But it was real. And in that raw, exhausted, barely holding on, I found Him, and learned to actually remain in His presence.

There were no crowds, no platforms, no filters. Just me and the presence of God. I learned something there I couldn't have learned any other way: that intimacy isn't earned by perfection. It's forged in honest surrender. In those moments when you stay, when it would've been easier to run.

If you're wrestling, you're not disqualified. You're being formed. You're being seen. Even if you feel like you've got nothing left, just remember; He's still there and he's not going anywhere.

Power of Fasting

Fasting became my act of war. Not just skipping meals but stripping everything away so I could cling to God. There were days I went without food, without comfort, without answers. Not because I was strong, but because I was desperate to feel Him closer. To prove He is stronger than my greatest weaknesses.

Over time, fasting became a lifestyle. Every Tuesday for five years. Four 40-day fasts on just water and juice. One year, I looked back and realized I had fasted 173 days. I'm not sharing numbers to impress you, but to show the depths of hunger that drove me. I was pushing my body, my will, everything to the edge. And yet, it never felt like enough. Because what I truly wanted was God's abiding presence and the life that only He offers.

When I fasted the weight on my soul was lighter and I lived more aware of the Lord's presence. I believe that the greatest growth happens not just by the passing of time but by time in His Glory. The more of the Holy Spirit's presence you live in the greater the transformation. Maturity is measured by how much experience you have living in Him. It's when living in Him that you actually get to know Him and what He is like, and everything else is just a byproduct of relationship.

Fasting quiets your body and your soul and it magnifies your spiritual senses making it easier to participate in what the Holy Spirit is doing. It's not that fasting causes more to happen, it's that you step into the spiritual dimension that you have had access to your whole life. There are some breakthroughs you only get when you fast. They are hidden riches for each person to discover that are found when you put yourself aside and you set your face upon Jesus. There are places I've gone and things I've seen that only happened when I fasted. I've witnessed outcomes that were a direct byproduct of sowing in fasting and prayer.

Fasting is kind of like making a deposit in a spiritual bank. You are saving funds to be used on a later day. Time spent building a relationship with the Holy Spirit builds trust and faith.

There always comes a day when you need to make a withdrawal from your account and all the time spent sowing into the Spirit becomes the foundation of the platform you have to stand on. By faith you respond out of the overflow of His trust in you.

"Blessed are those who hunger and thirst for righteousness, for they shall be satisfied." Matthew 5:6 (ESV)

Breaking Point

Most of the time there seems to be an ebb and flow to the Spirit during a fast. Sometimes a day has such beautiful revelation and you wonder why you don't fast more and other times you're fighting your basic human need to eat and your goal is simply to get through the day. The Lord always values when we fast and He doesn't waste anything you offer Him. Jesus is so honorable in how He responds to our choices that He'll walk with us down the very roads we choose and in His love, make them His own. Because He already chose us He goes ahead to ensure our success. *(See Exodus 23:20)*

One of the longer fasts I did in this season I went a full 40 days and didn't see a specific breakthrough I was contending for... so I kept fasting. Pressing into God and asking Him for movement. During this fast I had many dreams, and beautiful moments with Him. I saw breakthroughs happen for the people around me but He didn't bring about my third personal request. I started to get weary and discouraged with no indication of an end in sight. Then He spoke through a deep feeling on day 45. He said *"If you don't eat... you will die."* which is not the kind of response I was looking for 45 days into this process. I then responded with, "Isn't that... the point."

Isn't the point for me to sacrifice myself, pray and fast until something changes.

He said, "**You are trying to kill what I already died for.**" I broke down and realized that I missed it.

We are more valuable to Him than the promises we're contending for to come to pass. Our value isn't based on how we perform. Jesus already paid the price appraising our value. We are worth the death of Jesus. He paid for every sin and shortcoming long before we ever tried to earn His love. I was already His, but I kept performing and called it sacrifice, blind to the truth that I was already fully accepted and deeply loved.

We can't perform to gain what we were born with, and we can't sacrifice our way into greater value. We already have God's approval, and we didn't do a thing to earn it. It's a kind of approval no human could give, because only God could pay the price for it. All that's left is for us to receive it.

Like God

In Genesis chapter 3 Adam and Eve had a conversation with the serpent who was tempting them to eat from the tree of the knowledge of good and evil.

"Then the serpent said to the woman, "You will not surely die. For God knows that on the day you eat of it your eyes will be opened, and you will be like God, knowing good and evil." Genesis 3:4-5 (NKJV)

Adam and Eve believed the enemy and ate the fruit from the tree. What they failed to understand is that they were already like God. They were trying to obtain something they already had. In doing so they agreed to a lie.

I spent too much of my time striving for God to accept me and act on my behalf instead of living from a right relationship with right positioning. A poverty mindset, shaped by early experiences, was unknowingly projected onto God's character. Fear of missing out crept in, fueled by the belief that performance could earn what had already been freely given.

The Lord doesn't want you striving. He wants you resting in Him operating by faith that He is so good that He is bringing you into position to believe. You are already like Him. We need to stand in the presence of the King not as a vagabond striving for acceptance but as a son who is given it by birth.

After we accept Christ, by faith we step into our royal position which is to represent the King as sons and daughters. We are born into an inheritance into the Father's kingdom.

"Behold what manner of love the Father has bestowed on us, that we should be called children of God! Therefore the world does not know us, because it did not know Him." 1 John 3:1 (NKJV)

As a son of God you have benefits that sons have. You are valuable and accepted, you have access to the Father anytime you desire. You have the authority of His name by birth, and you carry His presence as an inheritance.

Our position as sons and daughters of God carries authority.

We don't just represent the Kingdom—we *carry* it. The world around us is meant to come into alignment with the greater reality that lives within us: heaven on earth. Jesus said, *"Do not fear, little flock, for it is your Father's good pleasure to give you the kingdom."* Luke 12:32 (NKJV)

We've been handed the keys. What we carry is not symbolic—it's transformational. Our identity in Christ isn't just personal; it's generational. The fruit of our sonship shifts atmospheres, influences culture, and reveals God's heart to a watching world. **You represent what the Father is saying to the world.** When He speaks, you respond. You hear Him even with all the noise, because His voice is the sound your heart knows. When you walk into dark places so does He, and when true power shows up everything else shuts down.

"Praise be to the God and Father of our Lord Jesus Christ, who has blessed us in the heavenly realms with every spiritual blessing in Christ. For he chose us in Him before the creation of the world to be holy and blameless in his sight. In love he predestined us for adoption to sonship through Jesus Christ, in accordance with his pleasure and will – to the praise of his glorious grace, which he has freely given us in the One he loves." Ephesians 1:3-6 (NIV)

The Breakthrough

During my fasting I had many incredible moments with the Holy Spirit and most of the things I prayed about happened. However I've noticed the Lord doesn't always answer things in my timing. Sometimes He can pick an unexpected moment to provide an answer to what you have been praying for. This was the moment of breakthrough.

Professor John T handed me the microphone. Standing in front of a group of Bible college students with simple instructions, I was supposed to ask for volunteers to help with the church's life development program. I was not there to preach or inspire, I was not there for anything more than simply asking for help from volunteers.

Before I could say a single word, I felt it on top of my head, and time stood still. The Holy Spirit was in the room and He was on me. When it started, it felt like liquid dripping on my forehead, as tangible as if water was falling through a leak in the roof. It dripped and wrapped down the sides of my face towards my chin. Every hair follicle came alive. This weight spread over, and pushed down on me. It seemed to flow like a wave but flicker like a flame. As it spread it intensified and reminded me of a protective helmet. It had an electric effect on my neck and shoulder muscles. It was wonderful and terrifying at the same time. It felt familiar but much stronger than anything I had ever experienced. It was like everything was activated all at once.

God chose that moment for my breakthrough. That was the more that I had been searching for the whole time. That moment, in front of the class with eyes all watching me, I stood unable to speak. For the first time realizing that our understanding of His Spirit is so minimal compared to what is available. We live in a tiny speck of awareness of Him, when there are mountains ready to explore. There is so much more of God's presence to experience and it is a journey worth taking. I didn't do anything for Him to show up in power. He just came.

This moment was similar to Elisha's calling where Elijah shows up and places His mantle on Elisha. Elisha had a foretaste of what He was to carry in the future.

When I didn't have any expectation from the Lord at that moment my fasting requests were answered not in the Secret Place but in front of a crowd of people. For a brief moment He gave me a foretaste of where we were going. His anointing was so incredible with such a mixture of expressions I barely could hold it together as my stoic nature melted under His awesomeness. That was a defining moment for me that has changed me forever.

The Lord satisfies our hunger with His presence. He uproots deep things that hinder our growth and ushers us into our royal position as co-laborers in Christ. He is calling us to live not as victims of our circumstances, but as sons and daughters who have a Father that hears, sees, accepts and loves them. *"The entire universe is standing on tiptoe, yearning to see the unveiling of God's glorious sons and daughters!" Romans 8:19 (TPT)* The universe has been waiting for you to reveal the manifest presence of God. Are you ready for the Holy Spirit to not only live in you but to dwell upon you? John the baptist said it nicely when He said

"Those who repent I baptize with water, but there is coming a man after me who is more powerful than I. In fact, I'm not even worthy enough to pick up his sandals. He will submerge you into union with the Spirit of Holiness and with a raging fire!" Matthew 3:11 (TPT)

We need the fire and we need it now!

Jesus said to them, "I am the bread of life; he who comes to Me will not hunger, and he who believes in Me will never thirst. John 6:35 (NASB)

7

Fire

"Whoever passionately loves me will be passionately loved by my Father. And I will passionately love Him in return and will reveal myself to Him". John 14:21 (TPT)

The room is quiet. Everyone is asleep but for you that can wait. Everything can wait. You sink into the chair, exhale slowly, and let your heart lean toward Him. Life is always busy but not now. You push off the list of tasks till a later time, because this time is for Him.

You feel something subtle within you that encourages you to try again. Pushing back a few yawns you pray and begin to turn your heart towards the Holy Spirit. Your breathing shifts into rest and time seems to slow down. Your heart comes into coherence, where everything is aligned. Your problems fade to the background in preparation for a single voyage.

The spirit awakens and rises up within you and draws you inward. Your heart is open. The wall begins to change and melt like wax as He walks into the room. Jesus is standing in your space, filling it with electric energy. His clothes have this effervescent look like they are floating in a different gravity. He has a light about Him that He obviously pulls back so your eyes can adjust and make Him out. He is not very tall, maybe 5'9 which makes Him shorter than me. His beard is well trimmed and His face is kind. His eyes are captivating. They look hazel today but they change color from time to time. He clearly sees everything about me. His light brown hair has a few curls and it's not very long, He keeps it tidy and this time has it pulled back into a bun like He made the decision to keep it out of His face today. He carries this weighty presence, that feels like a hug that could obliterate me at any moment. He is all encompassing and beautiful. He has known me my whole life, and is the definition of what it feels like to be home. He can be anywhere at any time but today He is here to see you.

If you could ask Him for one thing and one thing only, what would it be? What is really important to you? Be honest and answer that question for yourself.

Pause for reflection...

If you were honest with yourself, the request you made was probably not what you expected. Some things in life are just non-negotiables. All the little things we want to change pale in comparison to things that really matter. When we see God as the granter of wishes we are trained to ask for frivolous things. When presented with a single request your heart reveals what's really important to you. I'm not saying He won't grant smaller requests. I'm saying we aren't asking for the things that really matter. If we prayed like we only had one shot and it had to count then we would pray like our life depends on it.

"This is eternal life, that they may know You, the only true God, and Jesus Christ whom You have sent." John 17:3 (NKJV)

The answer to that question I have been asking my whole life is to actually know Him. Knowing Him is everything to me, because if I know Him then I know everything else is going to be ok. He is the one constant in my life that carries me through all the challenges. He always has since before I can remember He has been there, and I have a feeling He will always be there.

That is how He designed it, so we can have deep closeness with Him. *"I will never leave you nor forsake you." (Joshua 1:5 NKJV)*

The Secret Places

Since I was a little boy I felt this desire to search for Him. To search out places of quiet where I might find a way to talk to Him uninterrupted by the world around me. I remember I used to sneak outside with a blanket in the middle of the night so I could look at the stars and talk to Him. It was always so quiet so late at night. The world seemed to be on a pause from all the racing that happened all day. I remember one time the wind was blowing the tall trees nearby and they seemed to sing. I always wondered if the wind was some reflection of the spiritual world flying by but we just put it into a box of science without thinking more about it. As I laid on my trampoline I could see the vast milky way and talk to Jesus who always seemed closer in this context. This became one of my first secret places.

"But whenever you pray, go into your innermost chamber and be alone with Father God, praying to Him in secret. And your Father, who sees all you do, will reward you openly." Matthew 6:6 (TPT)

There are places you can go with the Lord that are like hidden chambers for connection, where truth is imparted, friendship is built and intimacy is cultivated. These secret places are discoverable and are required to build the depth needed to transform you into who you really are.

"But Jesus often slipped away from them and went into the wilderness to pray." Luke 5:16 (TPT)

We live with only a tiny portion of what is available to us and are limited by what we know. But what if there is more to know? If we live our whole lives based on what we see we massively limit God and our potential in His grand plan. He has so much more to show you and experience with you than you will ever know. He has been around a long long time and He is still creating new things. He is the original source and creator of it all, and among all He created, He chose us to be part of His family. He doesn't need anything from us. He didn't need to make us. He wanted to make us because He wanted family. He created a creature that was like Him, that felt, that made its own decisions, that had all the potential in the universe and would still choose to love Him back, all the while concealing Himself into a mystery in order to preserve our free will.

Another secret place of mine was born out of a dream that I mention later in this book, but for the sake of simplicity I'll explain it as a campfire. I'm not an outdoors guy, but there is something about a campfire that is so ancient and intimate that it captures me. When I pray sometimes I see a campfire where I met Jesus and I go back to it in the spirit. There is this stillness that is required to allow myself to go there. It's the same feeling I used to have in my backyard under the stars. Sometimes we just sit in the quiet and listen to the crackling of the fire. I get a sense that Jesus likes the company. Around the fire is a place where we breathe, we let go of stress, He reminds me that He is with me wherever I go. Sitting around the fire helps me to surrender and be in the moment. There is something about just being with Jesus that makes everything going on in my life so insignificant while reminding me that I am the reason He does what He does. Surrender becomes a little easier and He becomes more discoverable. There are more secret places to meet with Jesus, and some are built out of the material from your personal encounters with Him.

"There's a private place reserved for the devoted lovers of YAHWEH, where they sit near Him and receive the revelation-secrets of His promises." Psalm 25:14 (TPT)

Touchable

Having personal encounters with the Holy Spirit should be a normal occur-
rence, as we pursue knowing God. The realm of the spirit is another dimension,
but for the sake of simplicity I'm going to call it the spirit world although it has
more substance than our own. The spirit world is tangible and happening all
around you all the time. Although it is mostly invisible to the average person
it is still very real. We are not always aware of what is happening. But you can
train your senses to be more in tune with it. (Hebrews 5:14) There are more
realms of exploration that can be experienced with the Holy Spirit because
you too are a spirit man. You are part of the world God built and you affect it
with your words, authority and actions.

On more than one occasion I felt the Holy Spirit on me in a unique way. It
was a physical feeling that kinda reminded me of someone throwing popcorn
at my face and on the top of my head. The sensation almost bounces off
like an electric rain. At first, I thought I was mistaken and it was something
natural, but it has happened on dozens of occasions at different times. It
is like a smoldering that is happening in me as the spirit is rising up and
firing off ignition sparks. When I honor Him and cultivate intimacy then Jesus
meets me with His oil that is received in the secret place. When oil meets the
smouldering then you get a flame. The fire on your head can be the evidence
that your intimacy with Jesus is fueling the anointing you carry.

Refining Your Flame

Some days have different manifestations but for the most part my normal
daily experience with the Holy Spirit is like a pouring of liquid grace on me,
then the Lord sets it on fire, and then He fans the flame. It's a bit of a dance
where He pursues me and I respond to Him, and I pursue Him and He responds
to me.

The beautiful thing is He fans the flame often when we aren't looking for
Him but He also provides moments when He walks by and we have the choice
to invite Him to have a meal. Often I feel a simple touch of His presence on

my head or my cheek and it's faint but at that moment I have an invitation to a deeper relationship. (see 1 Kings 19:5)

In my pursuit of God's presence, I discovered that I'm the best version of myself when I live aware of His presence. I am the most confident and lifegiving version of myself when I am aware of Him. The inverse is true for me as well. If I feel dry and unaware of Him then I tend to fall back into old ways of thinking, talking and behaving. So my singular pursuit is to remain aware of His presence regardless of how I feel. His feeling overrides mine. In His presence my insecurities fade away along with fear. I feel empowered to go take on anything. The quickest and most impactful way to transform your life is to simply abide in Him. I am convinced that most, if not all of our issues would be solved if we simply remained in Him.

If you have an addiction that has pulled its chain on you repeatedly, go hang out with the chain breaker. Addictions can't go where He is, but you can. If your mind is plagued with voices trying to confuse or control you, go sit by the fire and let Jesus tell you a story. Those voices lose influence when you learn to listen to the one voice that matters. If you have trouble sleeping, go meet with Peace. He's a person and He will stand in your room and watch over you. If you are afraid to move forward, ask Jesus to carry you so you don't have to walk on your own. He is always available, no matter where you are. Since He gave His life while we were still locked in chains, how much more does He love you when you are trying to live right and on occasion... stumble? He accounted for it all. He is proud of you and He knows He is the only one that can get you where you need to go.

Where to Find Him

The easiest way to a secret place is through scripture. Scripture is layered with new revelation that has been unfolding for thousands of years. You can read the same scripture from one day to the next and the Holy Spirit can give you a different word that fits your current moment. That is because the Word is alive. Jesus is alive. He has deep wells that are hidden in plain sight for you to tap into any place at any time. Living in the spirit and reading the Bible with a teachable heart postures you to see mysteries and to discover doors to realities that are in the Kingdom of Heaven. Finding Him isn't really about looking in the right place. You don't need to perform to convince Him to show up. He is already with you. Unfortunately we don't always treat Him like He's in the room, or even invited. However He always wants closeness. It's more about training your senses to be aware of His reality. Jesus will show you where you can meet Him. *"Ask, and the gift is yours. Seek, and you'll discover. Knock, and the door will be opened for you." Matthew 7:7-8 (TPT)*

The other key to finding Him often is to do it with all your heart. *"If you look for me wholeheartedly, you will find me."Jeremiah 29:13 (NLT)* You actually need to posture your heart to wholeheartedly discover Him. That means being honest with yourself and being honest with Him. You need to live with a clean conscience, you need to ask yourself what is really going on within you. Your heart actually needs to be open and expecting a response.

When You Find Him

It is important when you are invited into a secret place of intimacy with Jesus that you leave all your baggage at the door. Your baggage is your agenda, priorities, your expectations of how God should behave. It's not about you. Trust me. You can take Him all your cares about today and your worries about tomorrow. You can lay it all at His feet and He will help you. Your list of demands and expectations don't deter Him, but they are also a distraction of what He really wants to do if you would just let them go. He loves you and will help because He is good.

Trust me when I say don't do that. When you are invited to a deep place, a rare place, know this; It's not about you. He is inviting you in for His sake. It's because He wants to share something rare with a friend and if you carry your baggage with you, how will this new place be any different then the one you left behind? Let it all go. Accept the invitation for His sake, not yours. He doesn't need people for anything but He wants us. He wants you to be with

Him where He is. (John 17:24). When you keep it simple and make Him the singular voyage you will be trusted to carry things that are far more precious than the baggage you left at the door. Sometimes you can't carry both. So sit before Him and be quiet. Be still. Be ready. And listen. Just listen for however long He wants. He has things He wants to tell you. Things that you have forgotten or even things you have never heard. Take a breath... just breathe. Listen... breathe again... Be still...Present your whole heart to the moment. He is listening to your heart beat just like He always has. Did you stop long enough to hear His heart? Did you notice His speed up when you walked into the room? He is waiting for you.

When you listen with your whole heart and you keep Him the focus then the Holy Spirit that is inside you bubbles up to the surface and covers your whole body. The Father supplies the oxygen or breath. Jesus supplies the oil because He is the anointed one. (see Isaiah 61:1) He covers you just like Him and when you are ready the Lord sets you on fire. (Matthew 3:11) They keep you burning and you just have to love them back. When you leave the place the Holy Spirit Fire stays on you. You can feel not only the anointing oil on your head dripping down your face like honey, but you can also feel the effects of the fire. It's not hot, it doesn't burn or heat you up, but it does flicker and move because it is alive. It dances to worship and responds to conversation about Jesus, or His kingdom. It intensifies with truth and seeks to break out on people. The Holy Fire is meant to spread. It burns down doors that you never thought would open and thaws hearts when they are frozen. It resurrects things to life that have been long dead. Before you realize it the Holy Fire burns up all the weight of the things that hold us back. He supplies us with the faith to take on anything. If God is for us, who can be against us? (see Romans 8:31)

The Holy Fire

The Holy Fire is the Dove I mentioned in the first chapter of this book and is almost a better picture of the fire because of how much personality He has. Imagine a dove flying in and landing on your head. Imagine its feathers gently touching the sides of your face as He gets comfortable. Imagine the wrestling of the bird spinning around to finally sit down to sleep. Feel the weight on your head and hear the soft cooing as He sleeps. Now imagine Him standing up spreading His wings out. Imagine the power He carries that repels all darkness. The fire bird is made of an eternal flame that purifies, empowers and invites us into communion with God. He is the Holy Spirit, and He is also God. He is the one Jesus carried with Him and He is the one Jesus sent to help you.

Since Jesus trusted the dove to you, how do you walk in such a way that you stay aware of Him? Successfully carrying Him requires a thought life that honors Him with intentional choices motivated by love. He promised to never leave us, but that does not mean He doesn't hide Himself inside you when you look at or say things that you should not. The goal is to remain in His presence and that sometimes takes sacrifice and obedience on multiple fronts even if we don't feel like it.

He Will Get You There

Jesus carries the blueprint of who you really are. He has seen your future and He is working on getting you there. He has a beautiful journey that He wants to walk out with you. It's not about a plan. It's about walking it out together. God already knew you were gonna pick Him. So He went back in time and picked you first. (see Ephesians 1:4-5) He knows what you're going to be like tomorrow. Good or bad He wants to be there with you. Jesus loves you, because He loves you, because He loves you, because He loves you. It's who He is. If you didn't change a thing, He would still feel the same way about you. He would still choose the cross.

You have been chosen by Jesus to know Him. (see John 15:16) He wants to show you incredible things. Secrets He hasn't told anyone. But He doesn't share secrets with just anyone, He shares them with His friends. (see John 15:14) Friends take the time to care about each other. It's a two way street in the good and bad times. If you accept the invitation to keep showing up then you have the opportunity to carry the manifestation the whole world is waiting for. The evidence of a true son of God. (see Romans 8:19)

Crafted Prayer: A Prayer for Burning Union

Jesus thank you for loving me and giving your life for mine. You are in me and I am in you. We are one. Lord manifest your presence in me and upon me as I enfold myself into you and ask to hide inside you. May I draw into the secret place of your burning heart where I came from and where I belong. I give you me as I am. I am yours and you are mine. Open the doors to the deeper places and overtake my reality. I receive all that you have for me today. I can't wait to get to know you.

8

Signals and Oil

"If you look for me wholeheartedly, you will find me." Jeremiah 29:13 (TPT)

Oil

On a quiet night, I sat in my bedroom, waiting for the Lord. The season had been one of the hardest I had ever faced. I left a ministry that had a major positive impact on me, to step out in obedience. I found myself unintentionally isolated in a foreign country with only my faith to stand on. I had one strategy for this difficult season... to pursue Jesus and the presence of the Holy Spirit. I went after Him every day with an unflinching resolve to live in His presence. I was determined to fix my face on Jesus, be still, listen, and wait. I took all my unanswered questions and threw them out the window.

As my music faded I sat quietly tuning my heart to the eternal, hoping for a signal. I was at the end of my limits and nothing else mattered; I was prepared to wait all night. I remember it like yesterday. It was Oct 5th, 2009 at around 2 am when something happened. In a quiet voice, I heard Him speak: "You matter to me, and I want you to know me." His words cut deep inside me and I was undone. I then felt it—oil drip on my head like there was a leak in the ceiling. The oil dropped slowly like honey down my forehead, and the reality of Jesus' Kingdom was tangible. My senses felt alive and my mind tried to catch up. I began to cry because He met me just the way I needed.

Spiritual Signals

One of the longest schools in my life has been determining whether something I hear is God's voice or something else. I want God to speak to me every day, but I also don't want to be afraid that I might hear something that is not Him. You may be like me, in that sometimes your senses break through the physical and pick up on the spiritual world. Sometimes you may *see things*, you may *hear things*, you may *feel things*, and that is normal.

I have had times when I have perceived conflicting information. How do we determine if what we are listening to is the Lord, our soul, or the enemy that opposes God, especially if the information isn't inherently good or bad? For example, I have stood in line at a coffee shop getting ready to order and I hear, "*I don't want you to have coffee today.*" It might seem like simple obedience is in order... but another example I have heard is, "*Don't help that homeless person today.*" The source of the information feels a little less obvious for the latter. It's easy to argue something is from the Lord when it is a direct quote from scripture, except when you factor in that the enemy knows the Bible as well. What do we do when what we are picking up isn't clear? I asked the Holy Spirit about it and He said

"*You hear things because you are a spiritual being, regardless of whether I'm speaking.*" I realized my ears were working just fine, the issue is not whether I'm hearing, it's whether what I'm hearing is coming from the correct source. What you hear is not the most important part. What matters is who is speaking.

Wireless Signals - Hearing

Hearing the Holy Spirit can be illustrated like a cell phone.

The cell phone is designed to pick up signals such as WiFi. With that connection, we can receive information such as a website, music, images, etc. With Wifi we have a limited range. As long as we stay near an internet hub we can get information. However, WiFi won't help if we're lost and away from basic civilization.

73

When we become a believer and are filled with the Holy Spirit we get a data connection. That data connection isn't tethered to the towers of this world, it's connected to a satellite in a different realm altogether. With the Holy Spirit, we sync to the kingdom of Christ and His Father when we pray, go to church, worship, and connect with good things built on good thoughts. If we are not pointing at Jesus then we will pick up signals from other bandwidths because we are spiritual in nature.

Our spiritual cell phones are upgraded and we learn to send emails or prayers to God. We can download software updates when we attend church, or learn something new about God. While we're connected to the right signal our personal apps or gifts work better. We can make phone calls across the planet and even share things with other people. Our dialog with God is instantly available because we have unlimited text messages or on occasion, we can get an encounter and have some face time.

In contrast, when we go out of the bounds of our service area our phone can go on roaming data. This is what happens when we are not connected to the correct source. We no longer can be getting that same connection and we may not notice at first. The connection can be disconnected, slow, or hijacked by someone else. The enemy can be phishing for information to use against us. Our spiritual phone can unintentionally re-sync to an earthly tower that isn't pointed to heaven. Not being connected to the right source drastically affects our ability to not only download data but to even interpret it.

We need a spiritual phone that syncs to cloud storage via satellite. The Holy Spirit is the signal and Jesus is the satellite that connects us to the cloud which is stored in the heart of God. The Holy Spirit filters the noise, decodes the signal, and sends us what we need when we need it. We need to stay connected to the source of life and let Him build history and trust with us.

Mixed Messages - Enemy Tactic

One day I was at work and I was feeling pretty nauseous. My brain went down the list of possible reasons like, Water intake? Did I eat something bad? Did I do something wrong? Then my natural impulse was to go get ibuprofen.

Then I heard a voice and it said: "*I can take care of that*". It felt off and I realized the voice was not the Holy Spirit. I know Jesus heals but that wasn't Him either. The enemy tried to imitate the Lord by offering me something that the Lord does but required that I accept it from the wrong source. I rebuked the enemy spirit by aligning with the truth that there was nothing wrong with me. I discerned the trap. I'm not going to accept a sickness so I can be healed of it. Jesus already paid the price when He shed His blood for me. There was no natural reason for me to feel nauseous that day. When I rebuked the enemy, the nausea left immediately and the Holy Spirit surrounded me like a blanket for the rest of the day. Don't hear me wrong. I'm not saying don't use medication. I'm simply demonstrating how a truth such as God heals can be cleverly wrapped in a lie and offered to us from the wrong source. The enemy goes incognito and tries to counterfeit what the Holy Spirit does to manipulate us into accepting a fake connection. Then we learn to trust something that's not the Holy Spirit. We need the truth coming from God to be our only signal.

The Lens - Interpreting

We all have a spiritual lens on our eyes through which we interpret the signals we receive. The healthier we are in our spirit, soul and body the clearer our vision is.

If our view of God is skewed then all the information becomes influenced as well. It's like having the brightness on our phones turned way down. It's hard to see the details. Let me give you some examples of how a lens can be distorted. Let's say God says to you, "*I'm going to give you some money*". We might think that's a good word. But what if we hear "*I'm going to prune you for a season*"? We might think, "Get behind me satan"! Although they both can be from the Lord.

To explore this further, let's say we have a foreboding view of the world. This is the perspective that something bad is going to happen to us just around the corner. Now when we get the information we view it through this lens, and we can't trust it, because everything looks bad, no matter how good things are. We can get all the right information but it makes no difference if our lens distorts it before it gets to our heart.

Our view of God and His relationship with us drastically shifts not what we hear as much as how we interpret it. Discerning the source of the information is only half the battle. The other half is interpreting the information through the correct lens. Our lens is positioned and maintained because of the history we make every day when we walk with the Lord in His presence. It is also fine-tuned by Jesus while reading scripture. The correct interpretation is always hopeful. It has attributes like *"love, joy, peace, patience, longsuffering, kindness, goodness, faithfulness, gentleness, self-control." (see Galations 5:22-23)* History is built over time in different kinds of situations where He might express Himself differently than we expect. We can be expecting Him to tell us something and He instead shows us, or touches us. God is Spirit and He communicates in various ways because He is creative like we are. He can talk however He wants.

Oil Continued

In a quiet voice I heard Him speak. "You matter to me, and I want you to know me." Then I felt oil dripping on my head as if there was a leak in the ceiling. I could not see the oil but I felt it on my head running down my temples onto my cheeks. His words spoke deeply and shifted something inside me, but the tangible feeling of oil took me to a whole new level of encounter. The source was true and my lens was clear.

With His anointing shifting the atmosphere, the need to perform for acceptance died. He spoke into my pain and reminded me of my value. He trusted me with His anointing. There was no excuse and no lie that could undo what I experienced. In the words of Paul *"Yes, everything else is worthless when compared with the infinite value of knowing Christ Jesus my Lord. For His sake*

I have discarded everything else, counting it all as garbage, so that I could gain Christ." Philippians 3:8 (TPT)

The Physical Anointing

Our bodies are built to experience God in different ways, We can hear Him, we can see Him and we can even touch Him. In my encounter I could physically feel oil on my head, not for a brief moment, but for months I could feel it. Day in and day out His anointing oil rested on my head and dripped down my brow. I had no idea it was even possible to know His presence in this way. I felt so honored by the Lord. Even with no knowledge of the correct way to carry it I was determined to protect it at all costs.

What is Spiritual Oil?

The term anointing means "to smear or rub with oil" (Oxford Dictionary).

It is used throughout scripture to represent the Holy Spirit. The Holy Spirit was in Jesus and upon Him. (see John 1:32) *Acts 10:38 (NLT) says, "God anointed Jesus of Nazareth with the Holy Spirit and with power. Then Jesus went around doing good and healing all who were oppressed by the devil, for God was with Him."* The word oil has a connection to the oil of joy, healing, provision, and favor. (Psalm 45:17, James 5:14, 2 Kings 4). Jesus is the source of the oil.

Who Gets the Oil?

In the Old Testament, the anointing oil was for kings, priests, and prophets. But in the New Testament, Jesus changed the paradigm by choosing nobodies. If He chose fishermen and tax collectors then the qualification is not based on earthly position but based on the fact that Jesus simply chooses us. Jesus modeled the importance of being filled with the Spirit by saying, *"Now I will send the Holy Spirit, just as my Father promised. But stay here in the city until the Holy Spirit comes and fills you with power from heaven." Luke 24:49 (NLT)*

It is God's heart that every single person that wanted to be anointed by the

Holy Spirit could have it. God could have required expensive things like gold as payment but He wanted it accessible not just to the rich but to the poor. His anointing is for everyone. Oil can't be easily removed, it sticks around, and God wanted something that would remain.

Purpose of the Anointing

"But you have an anointing from the Holy One." 1 John 2:20 (NIV)

Being filled with the Spirit at salvation is like signing up for membership. Being given an anointing from the Holy One is like being set apart for service. It invites us into knowing His nature and heart as well as empowering us to walk in our giftings and accomplish our calling. Salvation gives authority back to you but when we receive an anointing we get the power to be like Jesus. *"But the wonderful anointing you have received from God is so much greater than their deception and now lives in you. There's no need for anyone to keep teaching you. His anointing teaches you all that you need to know, for it will lead you to truth, not a counterfeit. So just as the anointing has taught you, remain in Him."* 1 John 2:27 (TPT). That word "remain" is the same word Jesus mentioned in John 16 which was to abide in Him. The anointing is for abiding. It's not a momentary experience, it is a physical manifestation of an inward reality. The anointing should be a constant source of oil for our lamps.

Oil in the Secret Place

"There's a private place reserved for the lovers of God, where they sit near Him and receive the revelation-secrets of His promises." Psalm 25:14 (TPT)

At salvation, we are given a deposit of oil to fuel our lamps. But in order to keep it burning we have to go get more oil. Oil is gathered in the secret place. The door to that realm is surrender. The oil is traded for parts of our hearts. It takes time to collect and patience to store it. The only place we can get oil is from intimacy with Jesus where we have the opportunity to become one. The oil we gather must remain pure. It can not have any contaminants from other loves like money, self, fame or false gods like entertainment or technology, fame, etc. The oil you get from Jesus is pure. It's full of His passion, His kindness, His faith, His joy, His favor, and every good thing. Guarding the anointing against contaminants keeps our connection clear and the power running. When we have oil stored we have the fuel we need for more intimacy. Anointing makes a landing pad for the Holy Spirit to turn up the flame that's fueled by the oil. Instead of just maintaining a tiny candle we can be a human torch that illuminates everything around us, fueled by the anointed one Himself.

The secret place gives you the opportunity to cultivate history in His presence. That history produces trust in His voice and His touch. The method of how you connect doesn't really matter. It can be through scripture, worship, prayer, community, a walk, and even through the gifts of the Spirit to name a few. What matters is the posture of your heart. Are you determined to connect to the real thing no matter how long it takes or what it might cost you? You don't need to learn about every other spirit out there to learn to recognize the Holy Spirit. When you know the real thing it's easier to spot a counterfeit. Recognizing the Holy Spirit speaking in a moment and interpreting correctly is accomplished by living in the anointing that is cultivated by time spent with the real thing. When we bend our hearts to Him it prepares a place for the Holy Spirit to land. In that secret place, He can share hidden truths about the world around us, other people, or even things about ourselves. Collecting precious oil is paramount for maintaining the intimacy level needed to keep your lamp light burning.

Practice Listening

Collecting oil looks like a relationship where we care about what He cares about more than our wants and needs. Take time to ask Him about what's on His heart, and expect Him to respond. Be intentional to give Him the opportunity to take over your scripture reading and the subject matter. It fosters a culture of discovery and lets Him lead things. If I don't get anything specific signal then I make the choice on the subject of the conversation. Sometimes He wants us to choose so we can participate in the journey.

Ask questions every day and write them down so you can revisit them. Lots of things I ask I get an answer right away but sometimes it takes some time. Try different varieties of questions and you might be surprised by what you hear. He always hears us when we pray, and He can't wait to respond. He cares about the little things just as much as we do. Prioritize Him and He just takes care of our concerns, because friends influence one another and they would lay down each their lives for one another.

The Next Day

That night when I heard Him speak and felt His touch I realized how little I knew Him. But when I woke up the next morning and that liquid feeling was still on my head I knew His invitation was real. For months I felt the oil on my head. When I slept I still felt Him. When I ate I still felt Him. When I cried I still felt Him. The encounter remained. It was the first time I realized that I didn't understand what it means to abide in Him. I believe there is an invitation for lovers of God to encounter Him and to know Him.

"This is the way to have eternal life, to know you, the only true God, and Jesus Christ, the one you sent to earth". John 17:3 (TPT)

9

Promises in the Desert

"In the last days,' God says, 'I will pour out my Spirit upon all people. Your sons and daughters will prophesy. Your young men will see visions, and your old men will dream dreams." Acts 2:17 (NLT)

The night before I went to bible school in 2006 I had a dream. In this dream I saw a wedding napkin that was white, and engraved on the napkin was my name and a glimmer of my wife's name in black and gold lettering. It was written in fancy calligraphy. Her name was out of focus but it started with the letter J and there was something strange about the last letter. I didn't think much of the dream other than my mom had the same dream the same night. It wasn't till she told me the dream that I realized it was important to remember. I had this dream 4 years before my wife came into my life.

I married the most beautiful woman in the world. She is the woman not only of my dreams, but in my dreams. I dreamed of her long before I met her. I didn't always know it at the moment but as time went by the whispers of the Lord revealed that He went ahead of me and worked out all the details.

God had me in a process when I was overseas where He was preparing me for marriage. I had these prophetic dreams of what the Lord was going to do. I knew where I was going, I just didn't know how I was going to get there, or how long it would take. *1 Corinthians 13:9 (NLT) says "Now our knowledge is partial and incomplete, and even the gift of prophecy reveals only part of the whole picture!"* Even when He gives us only a glimpse, He still invites us into the process. As we walk with Him, He fills in the missing pieces, so that when it finally happens, we don't just believe it; we know it came from His heart.

Signs

While serving on the mission field in Korea, something strange began to happen. The number 11:11 kept appearing everywhere, on clocks, morning and night, on receipts with exact change, even on the sides of city buses. These moments weren't sought out; they simply kept repeating, day after day.

Often, the Lord can speak through numbers like this. When something repeats, it's usually an invitation.

11:11 often points to Deuteronomy, where there's a call to cross into the Promised Land, but in this case it carried a double meaning. For years, there had been a quiet hope for a wife, and the numbers began pointing to Hebrews 11:11 (NLT): *"It was by faith that even Sarah was able to have a child, though she was barren and was too old. She believed that God would keep his promise."*

A tension formed between faith and fear. Fear of being left out, fear that the promise might pass by. Friends were getting married, starting families, building lives. And yet, the waiting remained. I believed that God could save, heal, and redeem. His Word makes that clear. But when it was something I personally wanted, I wasn't sure if He would pull through for me.

Hope

In Genesis, Abraham and Sarah believed in God for a promise for years. However Romans 4:18 (NLT) says *"Even when there was no reason for hope, Abraham kept hoping—believing that he would become the father of many nations. For God had said to Him, "That's how many descendants you will have!"* Abraham against hope, in hope believed that God would do what He said He would do. Hope is a powerful thing. Hope is believing that even if you feel you don't deserve something it will still happen. It's a strong belief that something good will happen for you. Hope is the vision. Faith is the action you take to get there. With no hope you have no vision. If you can't see... How will you ever get there? Jesus is the hope. He is the vision. When you pursue His kingdom everything falls into place.

Prophetic Dreams

While in England, part of the fasting season was spent praying for a future spouse. If prayer was needed on this side, it made sense that she might need it too. During one of those times there was a clear word from the Lord and I felt like God was going to do something around Christmas time concerning my future wife. It was encouraging but it was still only summer so I held onto hope.

Three Christmases

When Christmas finally came, a small group of church friends gathered for a party to catch up and reconnect. Time back in America was brief each year, so hosting a gathering made it easy to see familiar faces and meet a few new ones. During the evening, a good friend introduced his girlfriend. We had a great connection and there was something special about her.

A few weeks later, the return to England came with some confusion. There had been an expectation that God would do something, but nothing seemed to happen. Unbeknownst to me, I had made an impression on her heart as well.

About a year later, during another visit to my hometown, I had the beginnings of a promising relationship with a friend. Together we went to a Christmas party for the Church young adults. My future wife was also in that room. She later shared that she saw me leaving the party and thought. "Lord, what kind of girl do you have to be to get a guy like that?" Little did she know that God heard her. Minutes later, the friend stepped outside and broke up with me. A week later I left for South Korea.

Another year passed, and Christmas came again, this time in Idaho. There

83

was a sense that a specific day held significance and required attention. My future wife came to another gathering at my home. We talked and played card games. We had a great time. By the end of the night, it became clear that there was something special in that connection.

A few days later, a New Year's Eve party was happening, and she was there again. There was a scene where she broke some glass sconces. She went and got the vacuum to clean up the glass and she joked to the onlookers "*How am I not married? I'm doing housework in high heels!*" In that moment a thought came to mind. *That sounds pretty good!* It's funny the things that get our attention.

Confirmation Dreams

The next week I made a point to visit the Italian restaurant where she worked. As I sat down in the booth, I suddenly realized I had seen this exact moment before, from that same perspective, in a dream two years earlier during a fast. In the dream, my wife was running around a restaurant serving people. She appeared only as a silhouette, but I knew it was her. The way she moved was unique, my server that day, moved the same way. I don't live by signs alone, but by the Spirit of God. Still, I knew this was a thread worth pulling.

A few days later walking through a Fred Meyers store doing some shopping, the Lord's presence suddenly fell on me. His presence is everything, and when He shows up, it's worth pausing to respond. I ask questions like, "Holy Spirit, does someone need prayer? Is your heart turning toward someone near me?" The atmosphere shifted, and it felt clear that something had changed. This time, the sense wasn't about others, it was personal. I had an impression to come back tomorrow at the same time. I checked my watch and took a mental note and continued my day. The next day, back at the same spot and the same hour, His presence fell again. And right then, she walked around the corner. I knew at that moment that I was in the right place and she was the right person for me.

As friends we were texting. A night or two later we found ourselves sitting in a diner getting milkshakes. We talked about life, Jesus, ministry, all kinds of things. She was a strong, independent, anointed person who loves God. She is different from everyone else in that she had this confident fearless presence. She didn't really care what other people thought about her. My conservative Christian background would say not to be out late but it didn't seem to bother her. She was free from false religion built on performance and full of great giant slaying faith. As we talked into the night, internally I asked the Lord if she was the right person for me? He gave me another impression that she was the one, and that together, we would get things done. Essentially that I would be able to walk out God's call on my life. We stayed up all night in the diner and finished our unplanned date with breakfast. After that day we just wanted to be in the same space. The timing was finally right, and three Christmases later, I was standing beside the one I had been waiting for.

Promises and Time

We live in a world where everything we do is limited to time. God sees time differently than we do mainly because He dwells outside of it. When He said '*Let there be light*' in Genesis 1, time was simultaneously created. Jesus is the beginning and the end. He's been in both places and has lived every moment in between. "*He existed before anything else, and he holds all creation together.*" *Colossians 1:17 (NLT)*

You are an accumulation of His dreams spoken by His voice into this time.

What's remarkable about Jesus is that He doesn't just make promises, He moves through time to fulfill them.

While people often crave instant gratification, God speaks promises that unfold over years. "*The testimony of Jesus is the spirit of prophecy*" *Revelation 19:10 (KJV)* so everything Jesus says is prophetic in nature. When He gives you a word or a dream He's speaking about things He is bringing to pass in you and with you.

Sometimes God deposits a word in your Spirit long before it happens. Then He sets out to fulfill the word and when His word comes to pass you recognize it. In hindsight it looks obvious but at each point of time you're still only seeing pieces and looking for the parts you're involved in.

Moses was given an assignment from a burning bush. In Exodus 3:12 it says that this is the sign that you heard correctly... *is that you will return to this mountain and worship God.* Moses confirmation was only given after he finished the assignment. If Moses had heard wrong and the message was not from God then he probably would have died by Pharaoh's hand, but if he heard right then he would only find out in the end if he survived and returned to that mountain. Some prophecies we don't know how accurate they are until we walk them out. Moses had to participate by traveling the path with God.

"There's a private place reserved for the lovers of God, where they sit near Him and receive the revelation-secrets of his promises" Psalms 25:14 (TPT)

Jesus' words are prophetic declarations for promised manifestations which are available for you. His promises paint a picture of not just possibility, but probability. Time bends its knee to faithfulness. He's already erased your past, He's present today and He has already been to tomorrow.

When You Know It's Right

I heard stories for years of how people found their significant others. Many of them involve a battle and fighting for love and for the other person and that's an amazing testimony but my story was not like that. By the time she was in my life I had already gone through the battle. I prayed for her for years and I believe that made a difference in the connection. Our relationship was just simply easy. There are plenty of things I have had to fight through but my connection to her was full of peace. The striving ended and when it was time... it was just time. All the signs the Lord gave me demonstrate how creatively He speaks, but with His peace so present there was nothing to prove. We just trusted the Lord to lead us and if it worked out then great. If not we would be okay as well, because our standard of fulfillment is in Christ not in each other. We were not in a relationship for what we could get out of it but for what we could give to it. Whether in a battle or not is not what determines if it's the Lord. His peace does. That's when you know something is right.

Dreams

This story is full of all kinds of dreams and it makes it special, but those dreams are only the ones I wrote down. There are likely hundreds more throughout my life where the Lord spoke in profound ways that I didn't record. He loves to talk! Writing your dreams down honors the Holy Spirit. When you're faithful with what He gives you, He often gives more. Writing down dreams that don't even seem spiritual is exercising your faith and revealing an expectation from the Lord for more. Jesus has a way of revealing Himself to you when you're truly looking and listening. He may already be giving you the answers to questions you've been asking all along.

There are different kinds of dreams. Some examples are healing dreams, callings, warnings, corrections, intercession, directions, inventions, and warfare just to name a few types. In dreams, the Holy Spirit speaks a different language, one rich with symbolism and layered with revelation. God hides treasure for us to seek out. If you have ears to hear and eyes to see, which means you have a receptive heart for what He's saying, then He can trust you to know Him.

I began experimenting with this and intentionally wrote down dreams whether I could interpret them or not. Whenever I remember a dream, I open my phone and jot down a quick note. Then later in the day I revisit and work out the details, learn about my dream language and pursue knowing Jesus. At first, I had one dream every few days. But the more intentional I was, the more dreams He gave me. After a year I had 177 pages, many with multiple dreams on them, and dreams began coming almost daily. Being intentional in our pursuit of God opens the door for more of Him.

We were married on 11/11 in honor of what the Lord did in bringing us together. That number has since become a prophetic symbol for both of us. It's now "our number". She sees it often, and every time it makes me smile. It's a simple reminder of God's faithfulness through every season.

Jesus goes into your future and ensures it will work out for your good. The journey may not always be easy or free from pain, but He promises to be there, especially in the moments when you can't see how the pieces fit together.

Beyond Time

Take a journey with me. Imagine a beautiful field that's full of all kinds of flowers. Step into that field and focus on a single flower. Notice its color, the way it smells, the shape of its petals. That flower only blooms for a short, specific time. It's rooted in soil, surrounded by greenery, maybe even visited by bumblebees.

God doesn't just see the surface. He knows every detail within that flower. He knows when the flower is thirsty. He knows how much sun it needs to grow the best. Not only does He know that flower but He knows every flower that has ever grown in that patch of dirt. All of them. Not only does He know it but He experiences it. He knows the soil, how long it's been there, and what had to happen for it to exist in that exact spot.

Now imagine God seeing all the flowers, all the animals, all the people on the earth at the same time. It's hard to even quantify how much He knows. He sees the smallest flower, but at the same time He sees the farther star. He has no limit. He sees everything about you. He was there when you were formed in your mother's womb. He was with you when you took your first step. He was there on your wedding day. He was there on your darkest day.

At the same time, He is already in your future, working out the details for your good. He is already where your children's children's children will be born, already preparing the way for them, already weaving His promises into their story. His love spans generations, and His plans for you ripple far beyond your lifetime. He wants you to know that He keeps His promises. His faithfulness stretches beyond your time, anchoring both your present and your legacy. And it makes it easier to trust that when Jesus says something, He does it.

"Never doubt God's mighty power to work in you and accomplish all this. He will achieve infinitely more than your greatest request, your most unbelievable dream, and exceed your wildest imagination! He will outdo them all, for his miraculous power constantly energizes you." Ephesians 3:20 (TPT)

10

Warfare Tactics

The Bridge

Around two in the afternoon, I was driving home on the highway. As I approached the Perrine Bridge in Twin Falls, I was cruising at about 60 miles per hour. The bridge isn't extravagant, it's a four-lane truss arch span built in 1976, perched 486 feet above the Snake River Canyon. It's one of the few places in North America where people can base jump. The area is beautiful in that rugged, high desert kind of way.

Just as I was nearing the bridge, I fell asleep. My truck drifted off the road and started to turn. Sliding sideways through the gravel, I was completely off the highway and just feet from the edge of the canyon rim. The problem was I was asleep and had no idea where my life was heading. I didn't realize how far I'd veered off the path.

Camping

By this point I have been married for a few wonderful years. I got what I asked the Lord for, a wife. The problem with getting what we want is we start getting comfortable and we stop moving forward. Our journey to the top of the mountain literally stalls out when we become complacent, and we set up camp on a level lower than what God had planned for us. We assume that it's safe when in reality it can be very dangerous. When we refuse to keep growing toward Him we're actually running away from our destiny.

Comfort led to happiness, but also to weight gain and declining health. Because of the weight gain, sleep became shallow, interrupted by the inability to breathe deeply. As a result my dreaming with God faded. My body began a slow spiral towards death and it went unnoticed. There was a belief that a normal life was enough. That staying halfway up the mountain God called me to was acceptable. As long as the bills were paid and my spouse's needs were met, going further didn't feel necessary. I fell into a trap because of the lies I believed about myself and as a result I hung the call of God on a coat rack.

The War for Control

Our world isn't what it seems. We live life in a physical world we can experience with our physical senses such as seeing, touching, hearing, smelling and tasting. Yet we also feel things with our soul. Our soul is our mind, will, and emotions. At times both the physical and the soul realm interact with the third part of our being which is spiritual. We are spiritual beings by nature. The stories in this book reflect that interaction with the spiritual realm and how it invaded my natural world. You can probably relate and have your own spiritual stories when something you can't explain happened. This spiritual world has been around longer than what we know.

We live in what is called the 1st heaven which basically is our physical world.

Paul talks about knowing a man who went to the third heaven. *(see 2 Corinthians 12:2)* A few verses later Paul reveals that he's talking about himself. The third heaven is the place where God, angels and heavenly beings live. Now that leaves a gap that stands to reason that there is a second heaven. The second heaven is where the devil, demons, principalities and powers that live in the invisible realm dwell. There are no demons in the heaven God lives in. Now the second heaven is here on earth and directly affects our world. There is a lot of evidence of evil throughout history whether we believe in God or not. Our world is multidimensional in nature.

Adam and Eve

In the beginning of the Genesis story. God made Adam and Eve sinless and they were told they may eat from the tree of life but may not eat from the tree of the knowledge of good and evil. Long story short the devil convinced them to eat the fruit, so they disobeyed God and believed the devil. What people don't always realize is when they ate the fruit they switched masters away from God. Man gave the authority that God gave them over this world to the devil. That's why Jesus had to come as a man to take back authority by dying on the cross.

When we were created the Word says we were made in the image of God and that we are very good. We are made with His likeness. We are given from birth the thing the devil wanted for himself. To be like God. God made us in His image then put us on the third rock from the sun. This is also the place the devil, the fallen angels, and other spiritual beings that oppose God come to reside. We were never meant to be controlled and manipulated by darkness. However when we believe lies about ourselves or about God we become a slave to evil and are susceptible to sin.

War

The enemy of our soul is not trying to give us a hard day. They are not trying to make sure we have a tough go at life. The enemy is trying to kill us. They want our faith and then they want us to be taken out of the mission for the souls of men. People pretend they can live in a perpetual vacation and ignore the fight. Others can be perishing around them on the left and the right and they are sitting on the sidelines complaining because they don't have enough social media followers. There is a spiritual war going on all around us.

"God is strong, and he wants you strong. So take everything the Master has set out for you, well-made weapons of the best materials. And put them to use so you will be able to stand up to everything the Devil throws your way. This is no afternoon athletic contest that we'll walk away from and forget about in a couple of hours. This is for keeps, a life-or-death fight to the finish against the Devil and all his angels. Be prepared. You're up against far more than you can handle on your own. Take all the help you can get, every weapon God has issued, so that when it's all over but the shouting you'll still be on your feet. Truth, righteousness, peace, faith, and salvation are more than words. Learn how to apply them. You'll need them throughout your life. God's Word is an indispensable weapon. In the same way, prayer is essential in this ongoing warfare. Pray hard and long. Pray for your brothers and sisters. Keep your eyes open. Keep each other's spirits up so that no one falls behind or drops out." Ephesians 6:10-18 (MSG)

We are supposed to be standing, not sitting. We are supposed to have armor on. That's because we can actually get shot. The enemy of our soul doesn't always come straight on, because of course it would obviously hit our shield. The enemy often waits for the opportune moment to sneak in and pretend to be on our team. The enemy which can be multiple spiritual beings working together want us to be comfortable so we stop training. So we take our armor off, sit down and stop fighting.

Enemy Tactics of the Battlefield

There are many tactics on the battlefield that the enemy tries against us. Tactics are rarely obvious because we would see them coming. Tactics can be done slowly over time, chipping away at pieces of our armor when we give in to tiny compromises. Each compromise is attached to a lie that is intended to get us out of the battle for good. Here are some of those tactics that I have run into.

Imitation

We are spiritual in nature, so we pick up spiritual things. Not everything that goes through our mind is from ourselves. A common tactic of the enemy is to imitate us. They are opportunistic and make sneaky moves to manipulate.

If they get us to agree with something that is not of God's kingdom then we use our authority and our power to build the wrong kingdom. If we operate out of a wrong view of ourselves then we don't reveal Jesus. We reflect the lie we believe. It's all a deception to hijack our authority because they don't have any.

If we are not aware of this we might think an idea and give it validity when it might not even be our own. Some thoughts are obvious, but others are meant to lead you the wrong way.

For example, let's say there is a person at our work that whenever they say something it rubs us in the wrong direction. When they are around we feel irritated or angry. Our new nature in Christ is not to be angry or irritated. But when they are around our vicinity we feel those feelings that are contrary to who we really are. Let's say we impatiently lash out with words. Our conscience then is triggered because it wasn't good. At that point we might feel ashamed because we did something contrary to what the Holy Spirit says about our character. The enemy not only makes us feel the original temptation but when we give into it, they follow up with a suckerpunch of shame. Then if we don't have a healthy identity we might search ourselves asking why we behaved that way when the origin wasn't us in the first place. If we think it was us then the enemy tears down our identity, we compromise and define ourselves by that bad thing which wasn't in our nature in the first place. This is the basic shame cycle the enemy uses to make us self-destruct, by attacking our identity, convincing us we're the problem, while He stands back and laughs as we fight ourselves. We need to believe who God says we are so when we trip we don't burn the house down and take days to recover.

"He canceled the record of the charges against us and took it away by nailing it to the cross. In this way, he disarmed the spiritual rulers and authorities. He shamed them publicly by his victory over them on the cross." Colossians 2:15 (TPT)

Introspection

Introspection can be a common place to get tripped up. If we search ourselves without a renewed mind we find things we don't like. Our self talk is a good indication of how we are aligned to the Kingdom.

An example of introspection would be... "Don't try, you're not good enough, worthy enough, or special enough. You always make this mistake and that's who you are. You're not a good person so why do you try." These are all examples of an enemy hijack bent on destruction. We conform to the image of what we are focused on so if we are looking at ourselves we aren't looking at Jesus.

Everyone is trying to discover who they are. We see it all over advertising with the message, be unique..be you.. but buy our stuff. We have this innate desire to be special, to pursue something great, because God made us to be great. Just like Him.

But the enemy convinces people that being unique is the same thing. Uniqueness is a counterfeit to kingdom identity. To expand on that a bit. The uniqueness I'm talking about is spread all throughout advertising. It's a version of humanism that isn't about being special its more about being your own god. It has no mention of being like the one that created you, it's more about you deciding for yourself what is good, and right. Celebrating that you are doing it your own way. In fact Jesus is the only way. Jesus doesn't want you to be unique in this sense, He wants you to be like Him. Free, full of power, creativity and joy.

We are being conformed to His image, but we need to discover what that image actually is. We don't get value by being like someone else. We already have enough value that Jesus would die for us. It's not an issue of value. It's an issue of identity. We don't have time to look at ourselves, when we're too busy looking at Jesus. We need to keep your eyes on Jesus and draw our identity and value system from Him.

Confusion

Confusion is a tactic that is common and can cause our momentum to fade. For example, imagine we made a mistake at work and it may or may not be our fault but we get blamed. Then we can find ourselves on the drive home talking about the problem. We talk about the injustice of it. How it's not our fault. Should we speak up and tell our truth and defend ourselves or leave it alone, and we talk ourselves in circles. As we go around we get more anxiety and we can even experience anger or sadness or a number of valid feelings. We need to make a decision on how we're going to respond. The only issue is the more we talk about our options the more peace we lose and the more worked up we become. We can use all the facts in the world to justify ourselves but we don't feel that rest we get when the Holy Spirit is involved. Then we realize that we have been talking to ourselves most of the drive home yet we are not closer to the solution. That's most likely an enemy spirit that is causing us confusion. We're trying to use our mind to reason out a problem when what we need is the Holy Spirit to bring a spiritual revelation so we can supersede the problem with a higher solution. It's solving things in our own wisdom when we need the mind of Christ. *For, "Who can know the LORD's thoughts? Who knows enough to teach Him? But we understand these things, for we have the mind of Christ." 1 Cor 2:16 (NLT)* Confusion is avoided when we stay in that place of trust and peace with God. Invite only the Holy Spirit into the conversation and set our hearts to find His kingdom perspective. We need to value His direction above our logical hypothesis.

Fear

Fear is one of those things that is all over our world. As I mentioned before fear is not the absence of faith, it's faith in the wrong kingdom. It's like the carnal man's currency that is used to purchase stagnation. It moves like a wildfire to infect the people's perspective and the quality offered.

Fear of Man

Jesus said all things are possible with God if we believe. We don't have to stay where we are. The enemy wants us to think we can't move forward and upward. Our friends and family could be pushing us to stay, when we know we should go. Sometimes that's with safety in mind, but sometimes it's because people around us are protecting themselves. It's almost as if as long as we don't pursue God then it's an excuse for others to do the same. However the moment we step out and dare to believe God has more for our job, ministry, relationships, or finances all hell can break loose. The bar gets raised not only for us but for those around us. Some people don't want to be challenged, because they like just enough Jesus to feel good while they ignore sin. However we are called to a high place. To not only be free but to live in fellowship, reigning with Him. We are co-heirs, predestined before the foundation of the earth to live in Christ without fault. (See Ephesians 1)

You are seated with Him in heavenly places ruling from a place of authority. *"For he raised us from the dead along with Christ and seated us with Him in the heavenly realms because we are united with Christ Jesus."* Ephesians 2:6 *(NLT)*

Fear of Rejection

If we are afraid of rejection then we're placing our heart on people when it should be placed with God. Remember... He is with us wherever we go.

Our faith should reach out for the heart of the Father in those moments of fear. When we connect to His love He fills us with courage and we respond out of that overflow. It's His love that fuels our ability to face our fears, because His love is more powerful and more fierce than we've ever expected. When we realize who is with us and that He picked us then what other people do or say won't matter.

The Truth About Fear

For most of my life, fear felt normal. I didn't call it fear, of course. I called it "surrender," "safe," or "obedient." I thought I was being led by the Spirit, or at least by my conscience. But looking back, it wasn't guiding me, it was ruling me. I made decisions that looked safe on the outside, but internally, they were laced with insecurity and self-doubt. I gave fear so much authority that its voice started to blend in with the voice of the Lord, and when I pushed back, it tightened the leash. "Be careful" it whispered. "Surrender" "Don't do that." And just like that out of fear of disappointing the Lord, I'd give up.

It was always a "no,"
No to coffee
No to breakfast
No to comfort
No to dreaming
No to applying for a job
No to buying a car I actually needed
No to standing up for myself
No to talking
No to confidence
No to believing things could actually be good
No to enjoying something "just because"
No to laughing too loud.
All the while, silence on the things that are actually destructive.

For years, I wrestled with the Lord about it. I asked, "Why do you always say no? I'm surrendering everything. I'm trying so hard to listen. Why does it always feel like I'm being shut down? Would you say yes sometime?"

I carried that question in my spirit for a long time. I began to observe how frequently the leash was pulled. Even while I lived in surrender to the Lord, genuinely trying to follow and wait for the answer to my question. In the long silence the King who loves me gave me a revelation that what if none of those times were Jesus, that would mean that this voice has been around for years and years. That would mean it has been pretending to be the Lord for as far back as I can remember. My spirit rumbled and I felt His presence rise in me. The Holy Spirit carries presence. Peace. Power. Even when He corrects, He brings life. He has never made me feel bad for anything. He is actually kind. But this other voice? This thing I had been trying to please for years was a master of disguise. The truth came out of my own mouth.

"Fear, I no longer need you to keep me safe."

That was the moment it broke and its tentacles untangled and let go. Fear had been masquerading as my inner voice or and the voice of the Lord. But it was neither of those things. And it didn't deserve the space it had taken up in me. That space belongs to Jesus who actually loves me.

It seems obvious when I say it out loud... of course fear can't protect us. But somewhere when I was a little boy, I had made an agreement with it. Jesus was so kind that He bypassed everything and imparted to me the truth and gave me the key to undo the agreement to a conversation that I can't remember. Jesus began to reforge those mental pathways into something far better: Freedom.

"For God has not given us a spirit of fear, but of power and of love and of a sound mind." 2 Timothy 1:7 (NKJV)

Distractions

Life is busy. We live in a world of constant connection to multiple social circles, events, weddings, vacations, pursuing money, planning our futures instead of living today. Filling the calendar up with far more than we need.

This is a tactic the enemy uses to distract us from slowing down and being still before the Lord. While all of these things have elements of good in them, when we are constantly going and not taking the time to take care of the things that really matter we move into spiritual atrophy. Our spiritual gifts that we should be developing and growing in, go by the wayside because we can be too distracted with things like work or entertaining ourselves.

When we do have those quiet moments it can be easy to fill time up with social media or sleep. The result is we find ourselves too tired to pray, read our bible or just spend time with Jesus.

On occasion I find myself hitting a wall where I have entertainment yet still feel empty inside afterwards. The temptation is to fill that void with more entertainment right? Our world is constantly trying to fill itself with things, because the world recognizes a hole inside itself. That place of emptiness can only be filled through a relationship with Jesus which is the Life.

Complacency

Sometimes it's hard living around non-believers because they don't know what they are missing. It's even harder to be around Christians that are camping in complacency instead of pursuing knowing God's nature and presence. People accept a small degree of Christianity that makes them feel comfortable and allows them to live in a degree of self-centeredness. There is a line between living for Jesus or living for ourselves. I think most people, whether Christian or not, chose themselves. They sign the membership to be a Christian but they never take up their cross and follow Him. They live their life right on the edge of surrender.

Complacency slowly numbs the soul. It can lead to discouragement or even spiritual unconsciousness. While we're asleep at the wheel, the enemy of our soul is working in the background, looking for ways to lead us into compromise. Often it's subtle with a series of small choices that pull us off course. When we lose sight of God's vision for our lives, we begin to break the promises we once made to ourselves and settle into a lesser version of our calling. Complacency blinds us to daily purpose and quietly steers us away from our destiny.

When we live in complacency, we reinforce a lie that detours us, a lie that says the fight for God's kingdom isn't worth it, and that we aren't worth it either. It whispers that even if we give our best, it won't make a difference. But the truth is, Jesus paid the highest price because He sees the immeasurable value in you. You were made to carry His presence, to push back darkness, and to live fully alive in your purpose.

Fast Asleep

Sliding toward the cliff edge. Fast asleep only moments from the end. My truck was completely sideways, skidding through gravel on the shoulder of the highway, heading straight for the canyon rim, but Jesus stepped in. I heard the Holy Spirit say, *"Wake up,"* and instantly, I did. Still sliding sideways, I acted on instinct, trying to correct my direction. Miraculously, the truck shifted back in the right direction and I slid back onto the road, missing the guardrail by mere inches. God spared my life that day.

With the Holy Spirit fire raging on me and adrenaline pumping through my veins I realized I not only fell asleep physically but spiritually as well. The enemy had set a trap to take me out and stop me from stepping into my purpose. That's what traps are designed to do, steal our future. But God wrapped His hands around me and protected me.

I had settled for less, compromised my calling and accepted the simple life in the desert. I accepted the limitations handed to me by culture, by friends, by family and even by my own fear. But deep down, I was conflicted. The world around me didn't reflect the Kingdom within me. I've not only tasted more of the Spirit but I have lived in the river, and no matter how hard I tried nothing else could fill that space in my heart. Not comfort, not distraction, not even good things.

We can have all the money, all the fame, power, influence yet still feel that core part of our life unfulfilled. The emptiness is only filled through a deep relationship with the Creator and His Son. That day, I woke up, and the Lord started helping me put away my camping gear, clean up the mess and return to the climb, towards His purpose for me.

Staying Awake

We need to change the way we think about life. It's not enough to just be saved. We have to make a decision to pursue His plans for us because they don't just fall on our laps. We have to partner with Him, exercise our faith and capture new ground. We can't just camp with our heads in the sand hoping nothing bad will ever happen. We have to pick a side in the war for humanity.

"We are destroying speculations and every lofty thing raised up against the knowledge of God, and we are taking every thought captive to the obedience of Christ." 2 Corinthians 10:5 (NASB)

We need to destroy the enemy's tactics and capture every thought and make them obey Christ. The key to changing the environment around us starts by changing the one inside us. The spiritual kingdoms of heaven and hell are attracted to what we think before we say anything. If we capture thoughts that don't align with the kingdom of God and replace them with the truth of the word then we correctly align our minds and hearts. We attract heaven to fight with us when we hold our ground. God's Spirit creates an environment within us where He then manifests His kingdom upon us.

Stand Your Ground

The enemy can come in various forms against you. The most common I have found are people in your life that say things that are not in line to what Jesus would say to you. Never lose focus of Jesus and His leadings. Listen for what He says to you every day even if you're not sure if it is His voice. Remember your History with God and use it to reinforce your faith. Track your journey by writing everything God has said as well as what you think He's saying now. If you honor what the Holy Spirit is saying then you will be given more. If you are intentional with listening you will hear Him clearer and clearer as you get to know His heart.

Write a declaration of who He has called you to be. Keep the vision in front of you. (see Habakkuk 2:3) Track your prophetic words and expect Jesus to fulfill them. Remind yourself of what He has said about you and revisit it often. Keep climbing one step at a time and prove to yourself that you actually believe what He says about you. Having a vision points your feet up or along the path. You don't have to know every step, you just have to keep climbing. Trust that God knows how to lead you. He has a way of getting you exactly where you're meant to be.

Removing the Enemy

The other form the enemy can present itself is dark spiritual beings in the unseen world. (See Ephesians 6:10-18). These are invisible forms that are directly trying to influence you. The accusations and traps of the enemy can come in various forms. There are a handful mentioned earlier in this chapter. The best way to deal with these traps is to get so focused on Jesus and His presence that when anything else shows up it's obvious. Keep your spiritual senses in tune and you will recognize the differences. Ignoring the enemy usually sends the message of how insignificant they are in influencing you. However ignoring may not always be the answer especially if the enemy is trying to get a foothold in your life. With the help and leading of the Holy Spirit you can do what Jesus did in *Mark 1:25* Command silence, reminding them they are bound and rebuke them in Jesus name. We need to stand in our authority and believe that Jesus will defend us by any means necessary. Beat the enemy by wearing them out. Stand in such a way the enemy regrets ever coming to your house. They don't have perseverance. Perseverance is a fruit of the spirit. What you carry is eternal.

Jesus said to the disciples, "I saw Satan fall like lightning from heaven. Behold, I give you the authority to trample on serpents and scorpions, and over all the power of the enemy, and nothing shall by any means hurt you." Luke 10:18-19 (NKJV)

Back to Climbing

There are appropriate times to camp and other times when we climb up the mountain. It's important to know which time it is because camping for too long is dangerous. There's a point where a camp becomes a detriment to our calling and destiny. Camping is meant to be temporary. A place where we tell stories, cook s'mores, look at the stars and dream. But camping ends and we stand up and we get back to the fight. The journey continues upward. We can't wait for others to lead the way. Some journeys we take are just between us and God.

Climbing the mountain is us partnering with God to contend for His kingdom to be manifest in our world. As we ascend, the price we pay changes. For some it's eating healthy. For others it's letting go of relationships we have had for years. The Holy Spirit convicts of sin and as we lay down our lives, pick up our cross, and follow, we become more and more like Him. We don't lay down the things that make us special, only the parts of us that hinder our relationship with Him. Anything that comes between our affection and Him is positioned to become an idol. Things like work, money, entertainment, food are solid examples. All these things have an element of Him in them because they are from Him. The issue is when it moves in our heart and pulls for our affection. There is only one person who is supposed to live in our heart, and He doesn't share the space. Not because he's selfish, although He would have every right to be. It's because He is so in love with us and everything that makes us special, that He is destroying the things that hold us down and slow our accent. *"Jesus told him, 'I am the way, the truth, and the life."* (John 14:6 NLT)

Into the Northwest

Around the time I began waking up, I had a series of directional dreams. In one dream, Jesus invited me into a hot air balloon. As we rose into the sky, I looked down and saw a map of the United States stretched out below us. We floated gently across the map until we hovered over Washington state.

Not long after, I dreamed I was in a city in Washington. Jesus was there again, this time inviting me onto a platform in front of a massive crowd. I was stunned that He would call me out from among so many, and I felt deeply honored. As I stepped up, the platform began to rise, higher and higher, until it stood as tall as a skyscraper, far above the street.

These dreams, and others like them, confirmed something I could feel in my spirit: a move was coming. And more importantly, Jesus would be leading the way.

11

Cloud

"Draw me into your heart. We will run away together into the king's cloud-filled chamber. We will remember your love, rejoicing and delighting in you, celebrating your every kiss as better than wine. No wonder righteousness adores you!" Song of Songs 1:4 (TPT)

"I prophesy to you eternal truth: From now on, you all will see an open heaven and gaze upon the Son of Man like a stairway reaching into the sky with the messengers of God climbing up and down upon Him!" John 1:51 (TPT)

New Realms

While in prayer in early 2020 I started noticing a shift. The Holy Spirit began resting on the bridge of my nose. The presence would shift down from my head and cover my eyes as if I was wearing glasses. This happened for a few weeks at a time. I had a sense that prophetically my nose symbolized discernment, and my eyes vision so I had a feeling He was unlocking something dormant in me and opening a door to something new.

We recognize the voice of the Lord in different ways depending on how we are made, what the Lord has unlocked, and what we have trained. Some of the different ways we recognize the Lord's voice are hearing, seeing, knowing, and feeling.

Feeler

People who operate as a feeler tend to sense in their feelings what is happening spiritually with people around them. We can pick up the emotions of others close to us as well as discern spirits that are affecting them causing the emotional pull. A mature feeler can gauge the spiritual atmosphere of a room and shift it with the help of the Holy Spirit.

There is another variety to the feeler called a sensor. This area is often given its own category, but I believe it lives in the feeler realm. Feelers tend to be limited to the emotional spectrum and I think the sensor is a feeler that uses their body and spirit senses to discern what God is saying or doing. An example of this would be smelling something like burning sulfur when there is no natural explanation might reveal a demon. Another example would be sensing electricity in the air which reveals the angelic, or heat on your hands which might point to healing. As with some of my stories in this book it might be obvious that my makeup is in the realm of a sensory feeler. I feel His presence tangibly in a variety of ways. The Holy Spirit and angels can tap on my ear or shoulder or other places to send a message. A Feeler is a glory carrier. Being aware of His presence is as important as breathing air. The great thing about being a feeler is you tend to be one of the first people to recognize when the Holy Spirit begins to move and when Jesus walks into the room.

Knowing

People who operate with a knowing get a divine thought or revelation that they know is from the Lord. This is more common with prophetic people that operate with words of knowledge and wisdom. Their fruit is often immediate and far-reaching.

Hearing

People who hear the Lord's voice tend to hear Him in the still small voice, in their mind, or even with their ears. Hearing happens in many ways depending on how the Lord wants to speak. We know He can speak audibly but it isn't the norm. When I hear His voice, it's usually just after waking from sleep. I get a phrase, a word, or a song lyric. Sometimes a song repeats in my spirit throughout the day, and when I recognize it and respond, that's the moment I step into an encounter. I add those words to my daily log and cultivate an expectation for Him not only to speak but to participate in revealing what He is saying.

Seeing

Seeing is where a person perceives mostly visual stimuli. Some examples include seeing pictures in your mind or the natural, closed or open visions, and dreams to name a few things. People who see tend to be very creative and often see the world in metaphors and symbols.

We perceive this partly due to the gift we are given from birth but I also think the Lord unlocks more gifts on our journey that are needed to fulfill our assignments. Sometimes the Spirit will turn down the volume in an area we typically hear, and He invites us to learn how to perceive His voice differently.

"But blessed are your eyes for they see, and your ears for they hear" Mathew 13:16 (NKJV)

The Blind Ones

In early 2020 something began to switch in me and my normal sensing seemed to turn down a notch and the seeing realm started to open. Around this time I had a dream that gave me insight into what was happening to me.

We were sitting around a campfire in a desert area surrounded by rocks, sand, and a few trees. Jesus was in our group. He was sitting near me. In conversation, the information came to light that a female member of our group had been taken prisoner. When Jesus heard the news He immediately stood up and left to go rescue her. There was a sense of urgency to go save her before the missiles were going to hit and she would be destroyed. I watched Him walk down the road and He was passionately angry. A tan-colored storm rolled in from behind and suddenly curled under Him and around Him like a shroud. He was harder to see with all the clouds around Him. He wore the cloud like a garment. I watched Him walk down the road towards a reservoir. In the center of the lake was a fortress on rocks. He walked the single path up to a man-made barricade. The fortress was surrounded by a few handfuls of people in uniforms. They had red crosses over white with medieval armor and they kind of reminded me of the Knight's Templar from an old movie. Except they were all blind. They were called "the blind ones".

Jesus walked up to the fortress and yelled over to the guys. "Hey, blind ones!" The men, being blind, heard He was there and stumbled around trying to gather to oppose Him at the barricade. Jesus said "You have my people. Let them go." Just then thousands of missiles of varying sizes and shapes started falling on the compound. Several flew by Jesus' head. There wasn't time. Jesus closed His eyes and bowed His head and time froze. The scene shifted like a movie scene with a counterclockwise movement and time reversed and I found myself with Jesus back at the previous day around the campfire. Jesus was so clever that He was going to change the outcome by going back in time a day and doing it again. Then for the first time in the dream He turned to face me and looked right into me. I was not just watching but I needed to participate. It was now my turn to try. I woke up.

The Cloud

I had a new revelation about perceiving His presence. I could see the clouds roll in behind Him and cloak Him and when He looked at me, I knew I was supposed to see in a new way. See the truth the blind ones could not and help free the church from its prison.

I had confirmation about what I had been experiencing and instead of operating in a "feeling" realm as I have been for years He invited me to "see." I have been tasting His presence but now it was time to see His goodness. So by faith, I started "looking" with my eyes.

During my prayer time, I opened my eyes and the room was full of a white opaque cloud. I physically and almost suddenly could see clouds filling the room. I had a sense the cloud was already there and I was just invited to see what I already feel everyday. If I walked away from it then it looked more like a wall of white fog but if I walked into it then it would be more translucent. The Lord opened my eyes so I could begin to see through the veil.

Over the next few months seeing the cloud of His presence became normal not only in my secret place but I see Him in other places as well. I was standing in line at Home Depot waiting to make a return and I glanced up into the warehouse and I saw the cloud roll in and fill about half the warehouse. On occasion, I see the cloud around people specifically. I see it in my house multiple times a week, and in my prayer room often. I've seen Him on my front porch when I come home from work. I've come to recognize that the cloud is an invitation into the unseen.

Signs in the Wilderness

The glory cloud is mentioned multiple times in scripture which helped me have a framework for what I was seeing.

There is a great example of this in Exodus 24:18 where Moses was at Mount Sinai and the fire fell on the mountain. God's presence in the form of a cloud fell on the mountain and God spoke, calling Moses up. Moses responded by walking into the cloud. On that mountain, Moses received incredible revelation for not only that generation but every generation since.

Moses would talk with God in the Tent of Meeting and when He entered the tent the cloud would hover at the entryway. (see Exodus 33:9) The cloud was a sign of the presence of God dwelling with man. The presence of the cloud is a manifestation of the Holy Spirit revealing evidence that Jesus is present. Just like how the Israelites followed the glory cloud in the wilderness, the glory follows Jesus. The cloud points to Jesus.

"And at last, when you see how the Son of Man comes—surrounded with a cloud,

with great power and miracles, in the radiance of his splendor, and with great glory and praises. Luke 21: 27–28 (TPT)

At Work

One morning as I woke up I had a thought about the health of a work colleague and I responded with a quick prayer, something simple. "Lord touch him and thank you for removing his pain, and making him strong". I didn't think much of it but later in the day I happened to run into him and I remembered that I groggily prayed for him. I recognized the Father was speaking about him and so I began to recount what happened to my friend and I re-prophesied my prayer to him. As I spoke I saw the cloud suddenly surround him like a cloak. It grew thicker for a moment and I smiled because I didn't expect to suddenly see him practically shining. My colleague went on to explain how he had been feeling run down for a few weeks and needed some rest and encouragement. The next day he bounced back to his usual self and even came back and told me how good he was feeling. It was very encouraging to see the cloud surrounding this man. I knew the Lord was in my friends encounter.

Jesus wants to bring His Father's kingdom from heaven to earth. It is the foundation of the Lord's prayer. *"Your kingdom come, Your will be done."(see Matthew 6:10)* It shows that the Fathers intent is to come to earth, and establish His glorious kingdom. It's working and He is taking ground every day.

In the words of Jesus... *"What will you do when I begin to unveil the heavenly realm?" John 3:12b (TPT)*

Unveil the Kingdom

The Lord wants to tear off any blindness so we can see our world from the perspective of His kingdom that lives within us. He wants us to move the marker of what is possible and step into a greater revelation of knowing Him. We are invited to know Him and to be His dwelling place.

"So when that day comes, you will know that I am living in the Father and that you

are one with me, for I will be living in you. Those who truly love me are those who obey my commands. Whoever passionately loves me will be passionately loved by my Father. And I will passionately love Him in return and will reveal myself to Him." John 14:20-21 (TPT)

That word reveal is only used in one other place in Exodus 33:13. It speaks of Jesus personally revealing or manifesting Himself to us. The Lord is ready to unveil the heavenly realm to us... but what will we do when He unveils it? Will we respond? Will we shift our mindset into who we are called to be?

"Loving me empowers you to obey my word. And my Father will love you so deeply that we will come to you and make you our dwelling place." John 14:23 (TPT)

It is His desire to be with us, and that we live in Him. Dwelling with Him. It's not really about Him needing us, it's about Him wanting us. Being with us is His reward for doing what His Father asked. God is so in love with us that I don't think we will really grasp the fullness of how He feels, but the closest measurement is His death on the cross.

Ride the Elevator

There is a kingdom not of this world that we have access to. In Christ, we have the key to the elevator that ascends to the place of His presence. Every day we have opportunities to get in the elevator and rises higher into the Spirit. Through prayer, we traverse dimensions and become enfolded in Him as we discover His nature and how it applies to us. With Him you can ascend. Here are some simple steps you can use to exercise riding the elevator.

1. **Remember who you belong to—and that He is good.**
2. **Remember a moment when you recognized Him—when you felt Him, heard Him, saw Him, or simply knew He was there.**
3. **Thank Him for any moment you know He was part of.**
4. **Focus on that moment, and what it means to you. Let the world around**

you fade into the background, and be present. Be still and bend your heart towards Him.

5. **Ask the Holy Spirit to come. He is always with you whether you sense Him or not. What you're asking is for Him to make your body aware of what is already there and available.**

6. **Wait... Wait for Him to show up. The Holy Spirit might rise up in you or fall down upon you, or both. He may drop a scripture in your mind or heart. He may not come how you expect, but wait expecting Him to connect.**

7. **When He comes thank Him.**

8. **Now talk to Him about something specific that's on your heart or something that you sense is on His.**

9. **Remain connected. Stay aware of His presence and go about your day carrying Him with you.**

This is basic prayer. Prayer is one of the easiest ways to step into His presence and build a relationship with the Holy Spirit and Jesus. Prayer shapes our world and calls things into existence that did not exist before.

It draws us higher into the heavenly perspective we are called into and it draws Him closer to His joy. You are His joy. Every mountain you need to move or miracle you are contending for happens through a relationship with the one who has the name above every name. He already did all the work on the cross when He conquered death. You just need to see who you are in Him and who He is in you. Then live from that place of deep relationship where you see the realm of a spirit as the greater reality.

Keep the Main Thing the Main Thing

Keeping a steady flow of the presence of the Holy Spirit is done by staying connected to Jesus. Jesus is the door that lives inside the heart of God. He is the king of the clouds and you live in that glory cloud every moment you carry His presence. He unveils the heart of His Father to the world and He shows us hidden things. Stay in that relationship and don't leave it for rules, performance, religion, or even if you don't understand. Keep the main thing, the main thing.

It's all about Jesus. Jesus is the Father's only sermon. Everything in all creation is held together by Him. (see Colossians 1) We don't serve a God that's disconnected from our world. He's woven into every precious moment of our past, our present, and our future. He is the single most relevant thing in our lives today. You can search the scriptures and our world today and you will never come to the end of discovering the truth about Him and His passion for you. The entire bible points to Him, and it's an epic love story of a God who loves people even when they don't deserve it. Jesus sees us for who we are going to be, not for who we are today. Then He treats us like that person, and then we become it. You are His dream. Jesus picked fishermen, harlots, and tax collectors and used them to turn the world upside down. Now that same Jesus invites you into His cloud-filled world. You are invited to see more than you know.

Jesus said *that He does only what He sees the father do*. (see John 5:19) So it's imperative that you are actually ascending and looking at what the Father is doing. How will you see Him if you don't look? I want to be a person who knows Him because I have been with Him. I'm prophetic because He is prophetic. I'm kind because He's kind to me. He lives in me and I'm being transformed to be just like Him.

You know He has more for you. It is time to seek, it's time to ask, it's time to knock and be prepared for the door to open. (see Matthew 7:8) He is the door and you are invited to partake.

Cloud Hearts

The cloud is an invitation. On one occasion I saw a cloud in my prayer room. It was like a mist that I suddenly saw around me and I sensed that it was already there but I blinked and could see it. I saw a hand emerge inviting me in. I knew it was Jesus so I walked into the cloud. It was a gateway into a heavenly reality and inside there were angels everywhere, dancing and having a celebration. Jesus was with me. I then saw shelves slide in, out of nowhere, and it looked like a supermarket. On the shelves were different fluorescent-colored hearts. Pink, blue, green, etc. More than I could count. Jesus said *"These are encounters with my people. You have access to any of them. You will carry encounters for them, and you will show them my heart. Here... start with this one."* He pulled His heart out of His chest and gave it to me. I said, "What do I do with it?" He said, *"Keep it"*. So I did what made sense and put it in my chest, unsure if it replaced or fused with my heart. Before I had time to ask anything, Jesus opened His mouth and a scroll came out. He gave it to me and I ate it almost instinctively. He said, *"Now you will have the words and you will have no fear about what to say"*. I asked Him for help in talking with people, so I could appropriately represent Him. He said, *"Your angel will show you the doors for people's encounters. Follow me."*

When I talk with people, on occasion I see the door to their encounter. It's faint, like a ribbon of light flickering in the atmosphere. I'll see it flash briefly near them and often near their head. When I see it, I try to move our conversation toward it where they have the opportunity to encounter Jesus. It is beautiful in that moment when they get it. I see the light open to them and their countenance actually changes, like they had this moment of revelation. I don't always successfully get them to the door of the encounter, but I know it is possible, so now when I see His invitation I just follow.

At this point you have probably already realized that this book is one of those gateways. It's full of encounters to encourage your heart to be open to the more that God has for you. This is your invitation to open the door to more of Jesus.. Do you accept it?

Behold! He appears within the clouds Rev 1:7 (TPT)

12

Lightning

"I pray that the Father of glory, the God of our Lord Jesus Christ, would impart to you the riches of the Spirit of wisdom and the Spirit of revelation to know Him through your deepening intimacy with Him." Ephesians 1:17 (TPT)

The Diamond

Imagine you're looking at a beautiful diamond. The gem has many sides, and they all work together to reflect every color we can see with our human eye. The way a diamond reflects light changes depending on its orientation and your point of view. Like diamonds, the Lord is beautiful and mysterious. You never quite know what you're going to see when you turn to look from a different perspective. I think most people spend years looking at one side and fail to realize there is more to discover. One cut of the gem shows only a small portion of the whole picture.

It is God's privilege to conceal things and the king's privilege to discover them.
Proverbs 25:2 (NLT)

Let's explore this a little bit. For example, we can know God as our shepherd. We hear His voice. He covers our heads in oil. He guides us along still waters and lays us down in green pastures. There is a huge revelation of the nature of God all packed into a few verses of scripture. However, in a different portion of scripture, you might discover that He is the living water that takes away your thirst (See John 4). So He not only is the well, but He is the water in the well. There are many facets of revelation that are worth discovering. You can spend years looking at one piece of that diamond and limit what Jesus has for you, or by faith you can turn it. You can step into more revelation by believing that Jesus wants to reveal it. You might be surprised in the end that it's not the diamond that turns but that you do.

Lightning Rod

One day I was driving down the road when I heard Jesus speak with a sudden impression. *"You are my lightning rod"*. I said. What does that mean? He said. *"Lightning is my word, prepare for thunder."* I didn't completely understand but just hearing Him was encouraging. I knew there was something new coming my way and I felt it in my spirit.

A few weeks later on 11-3-2019, I was at church and we were doing a prayer tunnel as we had before. The previous time was so impactful to me. I was very excited to see God touch people. This time around I was on the outside praying for people. As members of the church walked by I would simply touch their shoulders and pray. It only took a few moments before people began to encounter the Holy Spirit in a variety of ways. Some people cry, some people laugh, and some people shake and fall down all just trying to leave the room. It's really an amazing thing to see. Eventually, it was my turn and on the first step I took down the tunnel I felt His presence. I felt a vibration in my hand. I raised my hands up as I took another step, and my right hand began to shake violently unlike anything I have ever experienced. I could feel electricity going up my arms. I live in His presence but I don't typically show an outward manifestation. I'm the guy that's always standing after everyone else is slain in the spirit. This time was different. I was very excited to experience the Holy

Spirit in a new way than I had before. I could stop it if I wanted to, but I was open to whatever Jesus had for me. The quaking continued to intensify as I walked through the tunnel. When I made it to the exit I couldn't help but smile. The encounter lasted for hours and even at the end of the day, I could still feel the vibration in my body.

Even though the day was over the Lord didn't change the subject from what He was saying.

About a week after the encounter on 11-10-19 I had another dream.

I was parked at a preschool in front of a grassy play area and parents were hanging out with their kids. Benny Hinn the famous healing evangelist, and His family were in the grass playing games and having fun being a family. I stood by my car door and saw Benny Hinn walk over to me and leaned against my truck like he was taking a water break. I thought to myself, "Wow, I should have him pray for me or at least ask him an important question." But before I could think of a good question he just started talking to me and he began to tell me about how "Back in the day this minister hadn't been around long but he was leading a service and he impacted Kathryn Kuhlman so much so that she came down to the front for ministry in about 5 minutes. He was a very unique individual." Benny said that "he didn't know that arms got charged up, and the anointing would just go." He said, "he didn't know the spirit worked like that at the time."

In the dream, I said "*That is interesting that arms store up the spirit like a battery*"

That's when I woke up. I knew that there was more behind the manifestation of shaking under God's anointing. The dream prompted more questions but it encouraged me to keep pursuing Jesus. It's not always about complete understanding. Sometimes it's about a relationship with the Holy Spirit that likes to shake us out of our box to see the world from a new angle.

Responding

I had this sense that I have been here before, where an encounter happened and I should respond to the Lord. The first time I encountered the oil it caught me so off guard it scared me. I didn't want to repeat my mistake and be afraid.

The last time it took months before I was ready for more oil. I belong to Jesus and so I'm not allowed to tell Him no. It's not that I don't have free will, but when I decided that He was my Lord... did I mean it. We are supposed to exercise our senses to discern both good and evil. (See Heb 5:14) This vibration felt like it was from God.

Growing up I always thought God showed up and did something supernatural for a brief moment then left. But the reality is every time He pours Himself out it actually causes lasting change that drives our relationship deeper. How we honor it can determine how it lands.

So with thankfulness, I responded to the Lord and honored what He was doing. His response was with a simple thought, *"Do you feel it?"*

I became still and I realized that I could feel the vibration in my hand. I could feel the Holy Spirit's energy. It hadn't left, I was just less aware.

When the Lord speaks it's not random, it's done with intentionality. Your right hand symbolizes what a person has faith for. I think He already gave me the answer to my follow-up question before I even asked it. I wanted to see if He would put the vibration on my left side as well which has never shaken.

Over a few days, I would take a minute to hold my hand out ready to encounter the Lord. It wasn't long before I could feel the Holy Spirit vibrations in my left hand. The faith needed is similar to what we exercise when we speak in tongues. By faith, I practiced discerning the vibration in my body and it was only a few attempts before I could switch the shaking on or off.

When I pray I often feel the vibration and I choose to step into the anointing in this way. When I vibrate I see in my spirit, lights shooting around the room and I feel a blanket of His presence float down on me. It's almost like I'm clearing the airspace and preparing an atmosphere for more of Him. This season was the first time in my life that my body reacted to His presence in this way.

Lightning Rods

The vibration is a personal confirmation of His word, and that I was His lightning rod. I don't really think the point of it was all the shaking, although it is important. The shaking was a sign of re calibrating my body to be in tune to the sound of heaven. The vibration increased my frequency in preparation to catch His lightning when He speaks.

Lightning rods are positioned on buildings to catch and conduct electricity safely to the ground. In the same way, believers are the ones that are in a position to catch His words that shape our world. If a word does not hit the rod then it can be easy to miss His heart. Either way when lightning hits, things burn. It might as well be our hearts that receive the burning effects. Positioning yourself to be still, aligns your heart to catch lightning when it strikes.

Honor

You attract what you honor. Every time I recognize something the Lord is saying I write it down. Just the act of recognizing its value trains you to listen for the shepherd, and the more you honor the more you get. It is a complete game changer for how I fellowship with Him. Whether it is a bible reference, an impression from the Holy Spirit, a dream or even a possible sign. Record it. We live by the words He is speaking today. (see Matt 4:4) In the first year of this exercise I had 177 notes with most of them having multiple words and dreams within them. The second year was even more. You may have noticed most of the stories in this book have dates. That is because many came directly out of my journal.

When I first started, I would hear something every few days which was eye-opening, because I didn't think the Lord talked that much. I realized he's talking all the time. we just aren't expecting Him to speak so we aren't listening. At the time of writing this chapter I glanced at my notes in June and I had written a prophetic word, dream, or revelation on 28 days of the month. The point isn't to brag, the point is to demonstrate that He is talking more often than we think. It doesn't have to be fancy or wordy or complicated. Somedays can be a single verse or even a single word. There are no limits to how He can communicate with you. It's just an expression of a relationship. He wants us to abide in Him and to let His words abide in us. How can His words abide in us if we aren't listening?

Be Still and Know

One of the beautiful words I received around that time was a correction about using the phrase "I don't know." I always thought the phrase was helpful to communicate where I was at, but the Lord brought it up.

He said *"Don't use the words 'I don't know'. I told you to be still and know."*

I said, *"Why not?"*

He said *"If you think... that you don't know, then it turns off the Spirit of Revelation. Saying or thinking you don't know is believing a lie about your connection with me."* To be still and to know(see Psalm 46:10) is how we position our lightning rods to catch His words. The lightning is revelatory in nature.

When I don't have an answer instead of shutting down the Spirit of Revelation I practice being still. Because there is one who knows everything. I ask and I wait a minute and listen, Sometimes He drops it right into my spirit and sometimes He gives me a single piece of the puzzle. Often when life is busy I'll quickly write it down to think about later and He will still answer the question throughout the day. It's not uncommon to get an answer within a day or two. Learn to ask good questions and you'll probably realize soon after that you know the answer.

Knowing

Sometimes God speaks straight into the core of our being. It's kind of like the Lord is a tea bag and He is placed in some warm water which is us. Then the tea seeps into the water from the inside and transforms its flavor completely. Hearing the Lord through knowing is as if an ancient gate inside you is unlocked and the Lord births in you sweet tasty tea. Then suddenly you realize not only was He speaking and you know something you didn't know before, but the word has already infiltrated your whole being and brought transformation.

Secrets

"There's a private place reserved for the lovers of God, where they sit near Him and receive the revelation-secrets of his promises." Psalm 25:14 (TPT)

When you live in a relationship with Jesus it's not uncommon for Him to share secrets. One day when I was trying to find a hotel for my parents I stopped by a place that had some history to it. I was walking from the parking lot toward the front door that was tucked under an overhang like most hotels. I glanced up at the building and I heard in my spirit "Do you think the hotel will hold up in an earthquake?" I responded with a thought... " I think so." I dismissed the thought as just my imagination and I booked a room for my parents that arrived later that day. The next morning at daybreak a 4.1 earthquake shook the city and they had to evacuate the hotel for a short time. I still remember the quake throwing me out of my bed. In retrospect, I realize the Lord was sharing a secret with me. Had I been paying attention I might have engaged the Holy Spirit and participated on a deeper level. When you are still with the Lord, it positions your heart to hear His secrets.

Returning to an Encounter

Jesus demonstrated what was possible for a man that was full of the Holy Spirit and completely yielded to God. He only did what He saw His Father do. So if Jesus reveals something to us in the form of an encounter, gift, or a word then we have the opportunity to live with that grace.

"The secret things belong to the Lord our God, but those things which are revealed belong to us and to our children forever, that we may do all the words of this law." Duet 29:29 (NKJV)

If it has been revealed and you have faith for it then you can have it. You can always go as far as you can see. It's one thing to believe in something you have never experienced, but the moment you have the experience, you now have a choice to carry it.

You can return to an encounter. For example, let's say you go through a difficult situation and you need God's peace. You have a relationship with Jesus and so you ask for help and He shows up and covers you in peace. The next day when you wake up you might not feel that peace. You have a choice at that moment to become what you think about yourself. If you think you are tired and sad you will become that by faith. You have Jesus and the Holy Spirit living inside your mortal body sustaining your life as you become more like Him. Jesus said He would never leave you. So His peace can't leave you, because Jesus is the peace. So the error is not that the encounter left, it's that you did. It is easy to fall back to your default setting of wrong thinking. It takes time to retrain your brain to think as He thinks. If you believe you carry what He freely gives then by faith you can live in your past encounters. Once He sets a precedent with His grace you have access to that part of Jesus.

However what can happen in life is a variety of things that distract us, distort our identity, and tempt us to sin which can numb our sensitivity to the Spirit. You can't expect heavenly encounters if your eyes are looking at everything but Jesus. A reality shift is required and you have to choose. You give attention to what is important to you. Returning to an encounter is simply returning to that place of intimacy where you and Jesus were one. Encounters are birthed through looking at the person it is all about. As a result, you get to enjoy that unique expression of the Spirit. It is the divine invitation to know the most wonderful person who expresses Himself in ways you can't even imagine.

Keys to More Encounters

Community

Some encounters only happen when you're part of a community. I'm almost positive the electric vibration encounter was imparted by someone around the tunnel that carries it. You might actually carry the answer someone has been praying for... inside you. God always intended for us to do life in a community surrounded by people with the same heart and focus. He is all about family.

Steward the Seed

Build history with the Lord no matter how different or uncomfortable an encounter may be. Stewarding a seed is creating the proper environment for growth. Write it down and pray about it. Interpret what God is saying and apply it as if your life depends on it. Because it just might. Don't be concerned if you interpret it incorrectly. You searching for answers glorifies Him, and honoring Him with a response just invites more encounters. Jesus intentionally picks those moments as a gift for you and most likely for you to share with the people around you.

Risk

Take more chances. God is waiting to break out and touch people, and He wants to do it through you. You are a glory carrier. You already carry everything you need to love the people around you. If we could truly grasp that the power of the resurrected Christ lives within us (see Ephesians 1:19–20), then maybe we'd face our challenges differently. We might even take more risks. The kind of risks that could become the catalyst for someone to encounter the love of God for the very first time.

Mystery of More

Unraveling what the Holy Spirit is saying through an encounter takes patience and time with Him. There has to be a degree of mystery that we are willing to accept as we journey deeper with Jesus in search of His treasures.

There are more depths hidden for you to explore. Take a moment and imagine a bookshelf full of all kinds of books. By examining the books from the spine, we can observe subtle differences. We might see a title, author, and some idea of how big the book is. That perspective reveals just a tiny sliver of possibility. However, taking a book off the shelf and delving into the pages reveals the authors heart and offers a deeper understanding. I think there is this tendency to look at a book cover and talk about what a great encounter we had. We are so focused on one perspective of the diamond that we can miss what might be in the pages. It's time to ask the Word to speak, and If you be still still you might actually get to participate and catch the lightning when it strikes.

Ask, and it will be given to you; seek, and you will find; knock, and it will be opened to you. Mathew 7:7 (NKJV)

13

Thunder

"He raised us up with Christ the exalted One, and we ascended with Him into the glorious perfection and authority of the heavenly realm, for we are now co-seated as one with Christ!" Ephesians 2:6 (TPT)

"I answered you in the secret place of thunder." Psalms 81:7 (TPT)

The Mystical

I have already mentioned how God talks in different ways including Seeing, Hearing, Knowing and Feeling, but there is another way that isn't talked about often and that is the mystical. This method has been emerging since the beginning of the early church and is rarely mentioned and not well understood. It speaks to the mystery of God and to the idea of being one with Him. It leans toward divine union with God that may include a variety of manifestations outside even the Christian boxes. Angel encounters are normal to a mystic. Experiencing heavenly things like the throne or Jesus or the Father Himself are normal. Mystics break out of the religious box and do things like go sit on the Father's lap... they demonstrate a different kind of prophet.

Where a prophet communicates divine messages through seeing, hearing, knowing and feeling a mystic is one who lives in both worlds. Their focus is the heavenly first, which speaks of how things really are and they are fixed on expressing that truth in the here and now. They have one foot already in heaven before they even get out of bed in the morning.

A word from the previous chapter about being God's lightning rod shook me out of my own religious framework and set me on a journey to go deeper into Christ and His mysteries. Where before I felt lightning, I later had another encounter which I consider to be the thunder that followed.

God often speaks in ways that go beyond the surface, revealing truth through layered encounters filled with hidden meaning. In this chapter, I will break down an out of the box experience step by step, uncovering the mysteries He is drawing us into and showing how each moment carries a deeper invitation to walk in the unseen realities of His kingdom.

Subsonic Encounter

Six months later in June of 2020 I went to bed after prayer and I asked the Lord a question before falling asleep. I wrote, *"Would you upgrade my sight?"* in my journal. I fell asleep with His presence on me and slept great.

At exactly 5 am I was dreaming and I saw a toy starfighter. I saw several orange pieces being pulled off and those parts were exchanged for blue ones. Then I heard an audible booming voice, **"The weapons on your starfighter have been upgraded!"** I woke immediately looking around my bedroom expecting to see Jesus or an angel standing at the foot of my bed, and the voice continued to speak very loudly, **"Subsonic Booooooooooooooom!"** Then I heard the sound of a mighty wind that reminded me of a rocket taking off. The sound was heading east as it roared across the sky gaining altitude. I laid in bed listening to the sound fade in the distance and when it finally faded two minutes had passed by on my clock. After the incredible encounter I got out of bed to respond with prayer.

Life has many encounters of varying kinds. I shared multiple of my encounters in these pages where the Lord made Himself known. Everyone has different moments that are unique to them and are often undervalued. Jesus speaks to us in various amazing ways and sometimes understanding comes right away and other times the truth is hidden for our discovery. The Lord places subtle invites into deeper revelation on our path and He's waiting for us to value the intimacy that's required to unlock the secrets He hid for us. I think a major key is to linger and wait a bit longer. Take a word from Him and ponder it, value it, and search for the meaning. *"It is God's privilege to conceal things and the king's privilege to discover them". Proverbs 25:2 (NLT)* The Lord has hidden things for us to find that point back to a relationship with Him.

This is one of the few audible encounters I have had the privilege of having in my life. It's full of all kinds of symbols and messages that the Lord spoke to me most likely by an angel. I believe there is a message in this encounter that is not only for me but for the whole church. Let's dive in.

5 am

The encounter happened at exactly 5 am. The number 5 in scripture means "grace." Examples of this can be found in the Gospel of John chapter 5 which talks about the pools of Bethesda. Another example is when David took five stones to fight Goliath right before His epic showdown. (1 Sam 17) Grace is the enabling power to do what you could not do before. Grace is often translated as "gift" and the gifts are not earned but freely given.

Starfighter

The voice said, ***"The weapons on your starfighter have been upgraded!"*** This was the first time I heard that I have a starfighter or spaceship. Spaceships are designed to fly in heavenly places, above the chaos of our world. Spaceships have the capacity to fly at the speed of light, they fight bigger battles from heaven and take down larger targets. The starfighter is a perspective shifter. It's the invitation to view the world from heaven's perspective instead of our earthly one.

You are seated with Him in heavenly places ruling from a place of authority.

"Raised up in Christ the exalted one, and we ascended with Him into the glorious perfection and authority of the heavenly realm, for we are now co-seated as one in Christ." Eph 2:6 (TPT) This means we already live in two realms... here on earth and with Christ in heaven. We have authority to already be there. What are we waiting for?

Realize where you sit. Step up into the clouds, take your seat in Christ and live in two kingdoms. We are seated with Him in heavenly places while still navigating life. We are supposed to keep our heads in the clouds because that is where pure revelation of His kingdom really comes from. His heart.

Jesus revealed His Father's vision in *Matt 6:9-13 (NKJV)* when He prayed *"Your kingdom come. Your will be done on earth as it is in heaven."*

God's heart is for the Kingdom of Heaven to come to earth and for you to live in that reality. Jesus prayed that we would be made holy by the truth.(see John 17:17) and that it is the truth that makes us free(John 8:32) That word truth actually means "reality." We are called to live in the reality of His kingdom and carry His transformative power to our world.

Remember how this started with a prayer that the Lord would upgrade my sight? A spaceship flies in space and therefore experiences a different reality than being on earth. The location of the ship's journey is in a heavenly reality. Upgrading my sight or vision is viewing our world through the lens of God's heart which is heaven's perspective. To see our world like He does. To solve our world's problems with His thoughts to wear the helmet of salvation (see Ephesians 6) and think like Him and have the mind of Christ. (see 1 Cor 2:16) To see a world that desperately needs the Lord's presence. To see a world that needs healing, deliverance, forgiveness, transformation. Now let's be people that provide real solutions to our world's problems by viewing our world from His point of view.

The Weapons

Not only do we have a spaceship but we have weapons. We are not helpless to the conflicts of our world. We have weapons to get the job done. The apostle Paul outlines several of these concepts in Ephesians 6:10-18 (TPT)

"Now my beloved ones, I have saved these most important truths for last: Be supernaturally infused with strength through your life-union with the Lord Jesus. Stand victorious with the force of his explosive power flowing in and through you.

Put on God's complete set of armor provided for us, so that you will be protected as you fight against the evil strategies of the accuser! Your hand-to-hand combat is not with human beings, but with the highest principalities and authorities operating in rebellion under the heavenly realms. For they are a powerful class of demon-gods and evil spirits that hold this dark world in bondage. Because of this, you must wear all the armor that God provides so you're protected as you confront the slanderer, for you are destined for all things and will rise victorious.

Put on truth as a belt to strengthen you to stand in triumph. Put on holiness as the protective armor that covers your heart. Stand on your feet alert, then you'll always be ready to share the blessings of peace.

In every battle, take faith as your wrap-around shield, for it is able to extinguish the blazing arrows coming at you from the Evil One! Embrace the power of salvation's full deliverance, like a helmet to protect your thoughts from lies. And take the mighty razor-sharp Spirit-sword of the spoken Word of God."

Our weapons are truth, holiness, peace, faith, the mind of Christ and His unstoppable word spoken for each moment we live. By faith, wearing them all like armor, we stand. Applying the word to the encounter I can see that our starships have shields of faith that protect us from enemy blasts. Our spaceship has a navigational computer to think with the mind of Christ as well as a droid companion that helps us navigate when we miss it, which is the Holy Spirit. We can fly in earth's atmosphere but we operate the best while in space. We are in a fight against the rulers of this world and have markings of where we stand and who we belong to. Our starfighter is equipped with laser cannons as weapons. Those cannons are the words the Lord is speaking into our present situations. We use His word to destroy the works of the enemy. They are propelled by heavenly power and are backed by Jesus Himself.

The Sound

The second part of my audible encounter was very profound. The word "Sub" means "beneath the surface", and "sonic" means "sound". There is a vibrational sound below the surface that shifted something inside me and I began to resonate at a frequency that aligns with heaven.

The "booooooom" is a prophetic declaration of the explosive power of the Holy Spirit. I also think He did it because He wanted to get my attention, and make sure that I couldn't ignore it. It's one thing to have a dream with a voice but it's another to wake up and still have the voice talking to you. It's hard to dismiss a sound that lasted for minutes.

Our world is held together by the spoken words of the Lord. *"For by Him all things were created that are in heaven and that are on earth, visible and invisible, whether thrones or dominions or principalities or powers. All things were created through Him and for Him. And He is before all things, and in Him all things consist."* *Colossians 1:16-17 (NKJV)*

Everything is a product of a sound. Nikola Tesla is often quoted as saying, "If you want to understand the universe, think in terms of energy, frequency, and vibration." When you think about the Lord, pray, worship, or just seek Him, you vibrate at a higher frequency that is more in tune with the Spirit of God. Whether you attract Him like a magnet or you step into His gravitational pull, the shift in you is obvious. In His presence His signal becomes clearer and full of purpose. His sound resonates in a way that shapes our tangible reality, carrying the transformative power we need... yet He places it just beneath the surface.

Heavenly Reality

"Christ's resurrection is your resurrection too. This is why we are to yearn for all that is above, for that's where Christ sits enthroned at the place of all power, honor, and authority! Yes, feast on all the treasures of the heavenly realm and fill your thoughts with heavenly realities, and not with the distractions of the natural realm." Colossians 3:1-2 (TPT)

The Lord wants you to live in heaven and walk on earth. To see the world from His reality because you are already part of the mystery. Christ is in you which makes you actually like Him, able to live in two kingdoms and do the things He did. Jesus is God's mind made up about you

You have the power just below the surface to manifest His kingdom. Intimacy, identity, authority, power are all heavenly realities to those who live in both kingdoms. We are to be a people who expect the Kingdom of Heaven to arrive when we do because we represent what God is saying to the world.

"By living in God, love has been brought to its full expression in us so that we may fearlessly face the day of judgment, because all that Jesus now is, so are we in this world." 1 John 4:17 (TPT)

Follow

"Teach them to faithfully follow all that I have commanded you." Matt 28:18-20 (TPT)

The realities of His kingdom here on earth look like something. They look like healing the sick, cleansing diseases, raising the dead, casting out demons, as well as destroying the works of the devil. *(see Matthew 10:8 and 1 John 3:8)*

Following Him requires that we actually see, think and act by His reality.

There is no sickness in heaven, so we should draw the line for divine health. Pray for people not because they are sick, but so His stripes are not wasted.

Poverty is not in heaven so we should release wealth as a by-product of our relationship to the one who has all the gold and all the glory. Depression, suicide, and murder are not in heaven. Deliverance, freedom and purpose are basic staples of the kingdom of heaven. We carry the answers this world is looking for.

When our life has an obstacle that doesn't line up with the word of God, where are we putting our faith? It is by faith that we are proving the one who is faithful. Our faith directs our focus. We become like what we are looking at. What reality are you... looking at?

Jesus is the standard and we should not compromise our belief system to an inferior standard. Instead release His kingdom with your words and faith to see lasting change not only for your generation but every generation going forward.

Upgrade to the Next Level

I believe the Lord is calling His people to an upgrade. Go up a level and live from a higher place. Produce better fruit from His heavenly storehouses. We are called to drop the weights that hold us down and keep us from taking off. The world wants to pull you down and convince you that you aren't meant to fly, but the Lord has already called you to come up here.*(see Rev 4:1)* Take off and defy gravity and experience your divine destiny. Live in heaven and walk on earth. Know His heart and know His mind where all things are possible with God *(see Mark 9:23)* We were never meant to live with our feet on the ground but instead with our head in the clouds dreaming of heaven and what it means for His kingdom to come. Learn to live in two worlds from a place of revelation of His heart for this generation.

Jesus said I only do what I see my Father in heaven do. *(see John 5:19)* He isn't saying *feel*. He isn't saying what I *know* His heart to be. He is talking in a way like He actually *looks* into heaven and *watches* the Father to get instructions. When was the last time you prayed and instead of a mental prayer you went to heaven and *looked* at the Father to show you the answer? We might actually be praying wrong. Maybe the next time you pray instead of sending a petition which requires His mercy, why don't you open a portal into heaven and go get His solution and carry it back with you? That seems to be what Jesus is doing.

Before Jesus went to heaven He was already part of it. While He was still on earth He was healing the sick, raising the dead, casting out demons. He was walking on water, teleporting not only Himself but others. He could read minds and walk through people who were trying to push Him off a cliff. He was shapeshifting and changing His appearance, walking through walls and don't forget He could fly. So when He said you will do what I have done and even greater things He was setting the standard not the exception. As I am in this world, so are you.

Eternal Life

Let me challenge you with a reality of heaven. When Jesus says, *"Abide in me"* do you think He's talking about now, or after you die? If He took back the keys of death then why do we believe physical death is the only gateway to have access to His eternal life? If He says *"I am the resurrection and the life. Anyone who clings to me in faith, even though He dies will live forever"*... but then immediately says, *"and the one who lives by believing in me will never die." (see John 11:25-26)* then why do we think we have to physically die in the first place? Just because something is our common experience doesn't mean it's supposed to be. When you received Him did you not receive eternal life? Maybe Adam and Eve were supposed to live forever, but maybe you were too.

Maybe eternal life is hard to ponder at the moment so let me try another example. Do you remember when Jesus was surrounded by His followers numbering at least 500 according to Paul? Jesus just takes off into the sky and ascends to heaven. Why do you think He ascended in the first place? Could He not already walk into other dimensions? Why not open a portal to heaven and say, "Later folks" and walk on through. He did what He saw His Father do, and He wanted us to see it too. He wanted everything visible and invisible to recognize who He really was so we could get a glimpse of who we actually are.

Let us give up the small thinking we are taught in this world. Let Him be the force that pulls you upward into who you really are. Set your eyes on the realities of heaven that are discovered by looking at the Father. It's time for you to go to the next level. It's time to lay aside the compromises, excuses and fear that can keep you grounded. You don't need them. Take hold of the higher realities that God is calling us into and unwrap a mystery. He personally asked you to follow Him, so you have permission to do the things He did. Be His message of love to the world. Learn to silence storms, walk on water or through walls. Learn to be like Jesus and defy gravity.

There is a sound coming out of heaven looking for a place to land. It's time for the sons of God to awaken. Do you hear it? The world has been waiting for you.

"Most assuredly, I say to you, he who believes in Me, the works that I do he will do also; and greater works than these he will do, because I go to My Father." John 14:12 (NKJV)

"Never doubt God's mighty power to work in you and accomplish all this. He will achieve infinitely more than your greatest request, your most unbelievable dream, and exceed your wildest imagination! He will outdo them all, for his miraculous power constantly energizes you." Eph 3:20 (TPT)

*In the original experience, a specific name was used for the starfighter that closely resembles a well-known fictional spaceship. Out of respect for copyright and trademarks, I've chosen not to use the original term.

14

Olive

As I reflect on the moments I've shared with you, I realize that this journey has been about more than just encounters with God, it's been about His faithfulness in the most intimate areas of our lives. We've journeyed through seasons of struggle, learning to trust His timing and His ways. As we come to the close of this story, I want to share one of the most beautiful and humbling chapters of our life.

I married the woman of my dreams which I already shared earlier in this book. Our marriage has been filled with incredible moments that have far exceeded my expectations. However, we had been struggling with infertility for about eight years. The story of how we ended up together was a testament of God's perfect timing, so it wasn't hard for me to believe God also had a set time for our children to be born.

In November of 2018, my wife felt led to partner with God in a deeper way. She began working with a naturopathic doctor, facing fears about her health, age, and worthiness. What unfolded was not a quick adjustment, but a prolonged season of surrender, one she fought through daily at great personal cost. She came into alignment spiritually, and physically with no guarantees that heaven would even respond. She never gave up. She refused to let go of what God had put in her heart, and of what she knew was true. She is a mom.

About a year and a half into this intense season we received a phone call that things were going to change. A friend contacted her, saying she had a dream in which my wife was pregnant. The next day, she took a pregnancy test, and for the first time, it was positive!

The journey to this breakthrough was full of waiting, trusting and wrestling with unanswered questions. It was a season where the unknowns often felt overwhelming, but we tried not to dwell on what we couldn't understand. God doesn't owe us any answers. He doesn't always reveal the "why" behind our struggles. But sometimes He invites us into a deeper place with Him. I believe that one of the reasons He does this is so when the promise finally comes to pass we can stay at the depth we traveled to get there.

Truly Living

When you live in relationship with Jesus through the Holy Spirit, He pulls you into alignment with your purpose. That alignment is discovering who He is and in turn discovering who you are. You fulfill why you were made simply by letting Him love you and by responding to that love. If you never do another thing that is right in your whole life, then it won't change how He feels about you. He wants you to know He is available to be discovered. You can see, hear, touch, taste. and smell His world. He wants you to know Him and you are invited.

8 weeks later

Eight weeks into the pregnancy my wife started bleeding. I said a quick prayer and she went into a calm emergency mode that I'll never forget. I have never seen such strength before. While she got through to the doctor, grabbed the medicine, and climbed into our bathtub, I did everything the doctor told me to do to stop the bleeding, while she remained calm.

At that moment the Lord spoke to me and a verse played in me.

"I will reveal my name to my people, and they will come to know its power."

Isaiah 52:6 (NLT) I knew it was out of Isaiah, but it was not a verse I had read in a long time.

Emotion came over me as I tried to understand what I heard and reconcile it with what was happening at the moment. Seeing that I was starting to fall apart, my wife looked at me and said, "If God wants to give us a baby then nothing can stop Him." I felt her faith and was encouraged by her resolve.

After an hour, our baby tragically came out. For the first time in this traumatic situation, emotion overcame my wife too, as our dreams began to crumble. As we mourned the loss that day we tried to comprehend what just happened. It took us most of the day to just get out of bed. We went to the store and I bought a potted plant to bury our baby. As tears poured out we offered our baby to the Lord and trusted that He was still good. The plant was called "Earth Angel Blue Lilly". Seemed fitting for our baby.

The Journey

The journey through hard times can be a painful path. Things don't always turn out the way we expect or even close to what we hoped for. We can't always keep control of the path we walk down, but we can decide who we walk with.

It's understandable to think: if God is good why would He let this bad thing happen? One of my favorite quotes by Bill Johnson is, "*If you want a peace that passes all understanding, you're gonna have to be okay living in situations that pass our earthly understanding*". We won't always have life or God "figured out". Sometimes we have to let go of the "understanding" so we can live in peace.

We can't withhold ourselves from Him, or hold Him hostage to our requests until life looks the way we want it to look. God is good. Whether we "get what we want" or not. Life has moments of anger, moments of sadness, and often a slew of unanswered questions. We don't want to get hung up on what we don't understand. When you give something to the Lord that costs you part of yourself the sacrifice goes deeper because it's worth more. There needs to be a degree of mystery that is acceptable because we may not get the answer until we get to heaven.

When God Speaks

Two days after we buried our baby I was spending some time with Jesus. I kept things simple with no agenda and just focused on Him. After a bit of pursuing His heart, He changed the subject to my baby and spoke. This is how the conversation went.

"Your baby's angel is still here."

Often when He speaks, He has a way of inviting a dialogue.

"Why is the Angel still here?" I said.

"Because the job isn't done," He said, Now thinking about the ramifications of what He was saying,

I responded, *"Does she still have a baby... is she still pregnant?"*

He said, *"Do you remember what Donna said?"*

Donna had prophesied over my wife a few years back specifically about babies.

"Yes, I do, Lord. Donna said, 'I think God wants to give you twins. Go home and talk to your husband. It's not a sure thing'... what about that?" I asked.

And He spoke as clearly as ever:

"This is that moment... This is the part you're involved in."

"Wait a second, are You telling me she is still pregnant?... and I'm involved in some way?"

"Tell her," He said.

"She's heartbroken. Can I tell her later, when it happens?"

He spoke straight to the point and I could tell that He wasn't playing games:

"If you don't tell her, it won't happen."

I carried that prophecy from Donna around in my heart for a few years and never understood why Donna said to, *"Go home and tell your husband"*. I realized when His word came to me that night that I was supposed to know, because it was also my assignment for today. When you live in friendship with Jesus He shares His secrets and we have the honor to participate in the outcome through the words we speak and the actions we take.

I received His word and agreed to tell her the next day. I also asked Jesus for confirmation that I heard correctly, preferably from a person. I asked for backup, an entourage, or even some angels to help me. I needed some courage to step up to the plate because I didn't want to miss it. I only had one shot and the bat had to hit the ball over the fence or I was going to really hurt the woman I love. Jesus doesn't mind giving confirmations when the goal is to sync your heart to His.

Confirmations

I went to work the next day pretty wiped out from crying. I was preparing to tell my wife what the Lord told me but I needed a day to prepare to deliver it. Timing matters. I wasn't in any shape to hit a home run.

Only a few people knew we were pregnant and one of these friends was at work and they came up to me and told me they had a dream. They didn't normally share these kinds of things but today was special. The dream included elements like my wife and I, and an entourage of friends coming to support us. One of them was carrying our baby and there was talk of another baby. My friend had a dream and simply telling me was enough confirmation to set my stance. All the details were a bonus.

Stepping Up to the Plate

That day I stepped up to the plate and told my wife that in spite of the baby we just buried, she was still pregnant and the Lord told me to tell her or it would not happen. She responded very graciously. She was glad that I had shared my heart and said while God could do anything, she needed to focus on the certainty of closure, in order to process the pain and heal. Understandable. But I was glad I kept my promise in spite of the risk.

I would rather take the risk of hearing wrong and spreading Love than hear Him and not act. When the Lord shares His heart with you about another person it's a very sacred moment where He is being vulnerable with you. What you do with that vulnerability will determine how much more of Him you will get. When you protect Him He gives you more.

After the Word

Now that I opened my mouth I went into a waiting period to see if the word was true. I had moments of feeling like an idiot, and moments where I was proud of my courage. There were for sure a few waves of doubt over the next few days.

Remember how the Lord spoke to me with *"I will reveal my name to my people, and they will come to know its power."* Isaiah 52:6 (NLT) It didn't perfectly fit the situation which left a question in the back of my mind. I had to sense the Lord left a breadcrumb for me to explore. I had to track the verse down to get the second part of His message which finishes with... *"Then at last they will recognize that I am the one who speaks to them."* Now the word began to make sense. There was another layer to this experience where the Lord pre-planted a seed knowing I would need it after the fact. He reassured me that He is the one who speaks to me and I can be confident in Him. He is so clever to speak the right things at the right time.

17 Days Later

Seventeen days later my wife went to get an ultrasound to make sure things had cleaned out correctly and we were okay to try again.

After a few moments, the technician announced,

"I don't know what to tell you, but you've been misdiagnosed. You are pregnant; by almost 11 weeks. Here is the heartbeat!" She could hardly believe His words. And yet there our baby was dancing all over the monitor without a care in the world. The simplest explanation was that we had twins, and God had held a baby inside through it all.

God still speaks, He is good to us and He's closer than you think. The journey is just as important as the destination. A moment like this miracle doesn't happen every day. God has more joy in stepping into our lives and doing a miracle than we think. His reward is more of you. He has all eternity to do whatever He wants but He wants to spend every moment of your life with you, just so you would know what love really is.

The Second Wave

At about 22 weeks into this journey we were feeling very confident in what the Lord was doing. We went in to get a routine ultrasound and the doctor gave us bad news. My wife's body couldn't hold the baby and we were going to lose her like we lost her sister. A joyful time turned into an emergency surgery to give my wife a cerclage which in simple terms is sowing things shut so the baby is encouraged to stay put. It was a waiting and praying game to see if the surgery would work. Everything seemed to work except for the possible doom the doctors gave if my wife started having contractions. They also discovered that our baby had a hole in her heart and more tests were done in the following weeks to confirm it. We held onto hope and we walked it out one day at a time.

By the grace of God, we made it to 37 weeks and it was time to have the doctor remove the stitches so that the baby could have room to continue to grow. What began as a simple procedure turned into a spinal tap that involved anesthesia. The surgery was a success, but in the process, they nicked my wife's spine which causes spinal fluid to not make it to her brain. As a result, she was unable to leave the couch because the migraines were so intense.

The Battle is The Lord's

On the third day after the surgery while she was laying on the couch in extreme pain the hospital called. They told her scans were showing something wrong with the baby's brain ventricles. That we needed to do more tests because it looks like the baby will need a stent put in to relieve pressure from the brain. My wife could barely comprehend what she was hearing as the enemy continued what seemed like a weekly bombardment of my family. She called me and I came home for the day prepared for spiritual warfare.

The obstacles in this season invited us to go deeper into intimacy with the Lord, and we responded. We continued to give our baby to the Lord and stand on the belief that He is good, and that our baby belongs to Him. The battle is the Lord's and we would not back down until we saw His victory manifest. The Lord spoke to my wife about not carrying the weight but letting Him carry it.

I rested my hands on her back and the Holy Spirit came in power. I felt the oil and the fire of the Holy Spirit on my head, a ripple in the atmosphere, and I knew God was moving. We prayed that the Lord would heal her spinal injury. That the Lord would fill the hole in our baby's heart, and regulate the baby's brain fluid levels. He holds the oceans so He can hold the correct amount of brain fluid. Then we prayed that the machines the doctors are believing would submit to the reality of the Kingdom of Heaven regarding our baby. That they would bow to the greater power that comes from greater authority. We had hope and His name is Jesus.

That same day her spine was completely healed and by morning the migraines went back to hell. A few weeks later my daughter was born. All tests showed her brain fluids were completely normal and the hole in her heart was completely healed. Jesus fills the holes in our hearts. Jesus touched our lives with His goodness not because we did anything right, but because He's good. It's just who He is.

Better Than We Think

What if Jesus is better than we think? Imagine the most perfect version of Him. Would He be patient and kind, full of unfailing love and faithfulness? He would never give up on anyone no matter what. When you pray He responds with angels to get things done. He watches over every moment of your life to ensure He's present. What if we consider the notion that He is really good? What if God is not only good but good to us? In the Word, Jesus healed everyone who came to Him. He never turned anyone away. Jesus treats people how His Father sees them, not how they see themselves. He calls out the best in everyone. Jesus has a radical love that turns the tide in the direction that no one ever expected. There is no one like Jesus. He is the singularity that is the perfect image of the invisible God. Maybe Jesus is better than we think.

Jesus has many apostles and prophets, but He doesn't have many friends. He is looking for true friends. He is searching through every generation for people who will respond. If Jesus walked through your wall and asked you for you... would you say yes? What would happen if you responded to His invitation? What would the world be like with a man or woman who completely surrendered to the Holy Spirit? Completely abandoned to The Truth? How many babies would live and not die? How many people would be changed for the better because of you? Are you the person He can trust to carry His dream? When you go the distance to travel to the depth He has for you, will you remember what it takes to stay there?

Show the world around you what it looks like to be a person who's been with Jesus.

"And I am convinced that nothing can ever separate us from God's love. Neither death nor life, neither angels nor demons, neither our fears for today nor our worries about tomorrow—not even the powers of hell can separate us from God's love." Romans 8:38-39 (NLT)

You're Part of the Story

Thank you for reading my book!

If this book encouraged or impacted you in any way, please consider leaving a review on Amazon. I read every single one, and your words help others discover the message too.

★ ★ ★ ★ ★

I need your input to make the next version of this book and my future books even better!

Thank you
Joshua Rinard

About the Author

Joshua Rinard is a husband, father, and a follower of Jesus who believes in the goodness of God. This book is not written from a ministerial platform but from a life of encounter. It is a love letter written from Him, with Him, and to Him.

You can connect with me on:

🌐 https://www.joshuarinard.com

📘 https://www.facebook.com/jrinard